SPEECH TRAINING

SAY IT IN ENGLISH
(T. Nelson & Sons Ltd)

SPOKEN WORDS
(Phoenix House)

GOOD SPEECH IN THE MAKING
(Rigby Ltd, Adelaide)

MOVEMENT, VOICE AND SPEECH
(Methuen & Co Ltd)

SPEECH TRAINING

A Handbook for Students

by
A. MUSGRAVE HORNER

*Senior Lecturer in Speech Education at Adelaide
Teachers College; Examiner in Speech and Drama
for Australian Music Examination Board*

A. & C. BLACK LTD
4, 5 & 6 SOHO SQUARE LONDON W1V 6AD

FIRST PUBLISHED 1951
REPRINTED, WITH CORRECTIONS, 1959
REPRINTED 1963, 1967 AND 1969
© 1951 A. & C. BLACK LTD
SBN 7136 0471 9

PN
4121
.H567

PRINTED IN GREAT BRITAIN BY OFFSET LITHOGRAPHY BY
BILLING AND SONS LTD., GUILDFORD AND LONDON

PREFACE

This book is intended to be a collection of information considered indispensable to the serious student. Controversial matters, better personally introduced by the tutor, have been deliberately omitted.

A considerable quantity of practice material has been included, not only to afford opportunities of applying theory as discussed, but in order to save a great deal of the time and trouble usually spent searching in anthologies.

The lay-out of the book cannot, of course, be made to coincide in detail with the normal order of class presentation. In some cases, therefore, the reader will have to accept statements on their face value until they are later dealt with in class, and he may, at other times, find incidental mention in the earlier class lessons of points to be confirmed in the later chapters.

Most teachers, in the writer's acquaintance, realise that ear-training must precede speech training, and are in the habit of devoting a short part of each lesson to "aural perception". A few minutes is frequently spent on a short talk, or paper, delivered by one of the students; inevitably, there will be some interpretational and expressional exercises, and from time to time various forms of dramatic activity. For such circumstances, where most of the lesson-time is taken up with practical work, this book is offered for use in private study, to supply a general theoretical background, to be qualified and amplified at the tutor's discretion.

A. MUSGRAVE HORNER

CONTENTS

CHAPTER 1

APPROACH TO THE SUBJECT

Before beginning a general study of Speech Training, the student will need to consider a short survey of attitude, to be accepted hypothetically, and to be modified as objective and analytical examination is systematically pursued.

There is no need, surely, for a case to be made out in support of the importance of good speech, especially for professional and social reasons. No proof is necessary for so obvious a fact that speech is involved in a great part of some, and in almost the whole of other professional activities.

Effectiveness of communication from speaker to listener is the only real criterion by which a speaker's ability can be gauged. There are many technicalities to be considered, but the end must not become obscured by these necessary means, neither must these means themselves become the end. Only when judged by effectiveness can alternative methods be compared and the better one adopted. Armed with this practical yard-stick, we shall see that the speaking of a clearly recognisable speech sound is of more importance than the ability to describe accurately the activity of the speech organs believed to produce it. It will seem less important that a certain tone-colour is beautiful; we shall be content if it is appropriate. Enunciation, we shall agree, need not necessarily be mellifluent, provided it is distinct in utterance. If speech is beautiful in sound as well as vital in expressiveness, so much the better, but effectiveness by which thought is audibly conveyed from speaker to listener must remain the criterion.

Methods of acquiring good speech must be sufficiently flexible to be adaptable to different individuals and classes under varying circumstances. Fortunately, there is wide unanimity of opinion on most of the fundamentals. Ear training is of supreme importance, and speech sounds and intonation should be taught by the method of aural recognition and accurate imitation. Physiological diagrams, and melodic indications on a musical stave, may be resorted to, but only in occasional instances where aural perception is exceptionally and obstinately insensitive, or as an aid to making an (always imperfect) visual record.

The technique of vocal expression should always be regarded as an analysis of the general means whereby desirable results are obtained in expressing imaginative understanding of a passage. The principles employed should not be regarded as the only rules by which a rendering can be expressively spoken. Interpretation must always be the result of mental understanding and emotional reaction. The understanding can, of course, be assisted by clear definition and explanation, and the emotions may be stimulated by appropriate suggestion. There should not, however, be any insistence by the specialist on his particular rendering being imitated by the student: such enforced imitation would result in the crushing out of all individual expressiveness. Interpretation must remain an individual and personal matter. Imaginative conception needs to be served by unobtrusive technique, but the mechanics must never be allowed to usurp their necessary but subordinate position. The foregoing remarks apply to conscious imitation; unconscious imitation can never be checked. Indeed, it is by imitation that all speech is acquired, and environment has a much more powerful effect upon the speech of a student than his comparatively short periods of more conscious speech training.

The question of "Standard English" is frequently

misunderstood by students who do not take the trouble to ascertain the specialist's definition of the term. For the present, suffice it to say that to advocate the use of standard English is not to insist on uniformity of speech, an impossibility in any case. Those who advocate a standard form of speech in general recommend only the use of the same sounds by all speakers of English, and the use of an agreed pronunciation. Their aim is intelligibility. The manifestation of personality in speech has little to do with the formation of speech sounds. Individuality and character are expressed rather by such means as tone, tempo, rhythm, pitch, and the general scheme of modulation, none of which factors can be standardised. The idea behind the use of standard English is simply to assist in the clear interchange of ideas when people from different districts have necessity to discuss matters of common importance. There is no reason why these people should not use their own local forms of speech under ordinary everyday circumstances, if by so doing their communication would be stronger in their normal environment.

Most speech specialists believe that local variants and dialects should be encouraged—for regional purposes— side by side with standard English for national purposes, but whatever our attitude, dialects are slowly becoming less extreme. Ease of modern travel, movement of troops and evacuation of civilians during wartime, broadcasting, the cinema and sound recordings are all having a "smoothing-out" effect on local differences. Whatever personal stand the student may take on this matter, it is almost certain that he will sooner or later realise the necessity of speaking a standard form of English on occasions when a regional variant would be unsuitable, even if he sentimentally clings to his dialect for everyday purposes.

Some form of indicating sounds is clearly necessary, if only to avoid ambiguity, and the student is advised to learn the recognised symbols used, where necessary, in this book. If he is not interested, he need not study the science of phonetics; in fact he need not even learn to use the symbols, but he will find them of great use in indicating pronunciations more accurately than the usual orthographic script permits.

Having agreed that the ultimate standard of speech can be assessed only by its degree of expressiveness, it follows that training in speech technique cannot be isolated from the subject-matter requiring communication. The concentration of thought in verse, and the characterisation involved in drama, supply intense stimulus to vigorous speech. Dramatic exercises are especially useful. Whether the character being portrayed is either instinctively recognised or analytically examined, it is surprising to observe how frequently inhibitions of speech are broken down, and how much more readily emotion seems to be liberated, if a student is required to portray a character other than his own. The clear emphasis thus acquired can soon be used "naturally" in his own personal utterance. Verse-speaking has frequently been abused by a tendency to strain after "poetic effect", and sometimes the use of short excerpts has been advocated to develop "beauty of sound". Whenever possible, the student should avoid using excerpts which are too short to indicate the atmosphere of the complete poem, play or book from which they have been taken, or his "expression" will inevitably become spurious and superficial. In any form of oral reading to an audience (real or imaginary) the student must develop the ability, not only to understand, but to accept the sense of the subject-matter. Without this process of acceptance (as a point of view and not necessarily shared by the reader) it is impossible to convey the content with true emphatic values and with a convincing impression of spontaneity in the application of technique.

At the beginning, the student must realise that speech habits are changing all the time, and "standards" require frequent modification. Moreover, there is still a great deal about the nature of speech which is not scientifically understood and it will be some time yet before an adequate psychological explanation of speech as a form of behaviour will be ours. The attitude of the student must, therefore, of necessity be experimental. The student should be prepared to consider and test by experiment and experience any hypothesis. Specialist and student alike must be ready to forsake any cherished conception which cannot be reconciled to the findings of modern research. New investigatory findings must lead to fresh methods—judged only by their effectiveness.

Lastly, speech may be studied anywhere and everywhere, and the work in the class-room or studio should stimulate the student to investigate speech activity in the world about him. He should, however, constantly bear in mind the fact that speech is a "touchy" subject. Tactfulness is most essential when approaching others— pupils, fellow-students, or colleagues—and objective criticism and frequent examination and analysis of his own speech is imperative if the student is to assess his personal standard of speech unbiassed by local sentimentality, false class distinction, or personal pride and prejudice.

To get the best value from this present practical handbook, the following order is suggested:

1. Read the book through in order to obtain a general view.
2. Repeat, but this time working on each exercise for its explicit purpose.
3. At the end, work through all exercises again, so that the earlier excerpts will be reconsidered and rendered with the technique acquired from the entire scheme of study.

CHAPTER 2

VOWELS

In speech, the outgoing breath is used to vibrate the vocal cords. This vibration is reinforced by the resonances of the mouth, the nasal and other cavities. As a practical definition, adequate for the purposes of this chapter, it might be stated that "Voice is the resultant sound produced by the vibration of the vocal cords, after it has acquired resonances from the several cavities through which it passes." This matter will be more fully discussed in a later chapter on "Voice Production". For the present the definition just given is a necessary starting-point for the following elementary consideration of Speech Sounds.

The most obvious classification of speech sounds arises from an easily observed fact. Even the most superficial examination of the sounds used in ordinary speech will reveal that, on the one hand, some sounds are the result of resonance only, the mouth being open sufficiently to allow free passage of voice. On the other hand, some sounds are the result of one or more organs of speech being used to obstruct or impede the outgoing voice or breath. The former are called vowels, and the latter are called consonants.

A simple experiment is suggested. Speak the word "all". It contains two sounds (there should be no confusion between letters and sounds), and observation in a mirror will demonstrate that this word begins with a vowel through a fairly free mouth passage, and finishes with a consonant caused by the tongue rising to touch the roof of the mouth and thereby causing a partial obstruction of sound.

Vowels depend upon characteristic resonances for their identification. To produce a required sound, mouth resonance is controlled principally by the positioning of the tongue and the lips, and it is desirable that this positioning should be unconsciously achieved. Some vowels depend mainly upon the tongue, others depend much upon the lips. It is easy to demonstrate this fact, along the following lines:

(1) Try to say the vowels only in S*EE*, P*ET* and *AR*THUR, deliberately resisting any lip movement. It will be a comparatively simple matter to give clear differentiation between the three vowels respectively.

(2) Repeating the experiment, this time with the tongue in a fixed position (checking, if necessary, with the aid of a mirror), it will be found that no amount of lip shaping can compensate for lack of tongue positioning. Quite obviously, then, the vowels in S*EE*, P*ET* and *AR*THUR depend mainly upon the tongue.

(3) If a similar experiment is now tried on the vowels as in T*OO*, C*OA*T and C*AU*GHT, allowing tongue, but no lip, movement. And finally,

(4) Allowing the lips to shape themselves, but resisting tongue movement, the vowels in T*OO*, C*OA*T and C*AU*GHT will be heard to depend largely upon the lips.

Fig. 1, showing (*a*) the approximate tongue, and (*b*) lip positions for the vowels in question, is given to illustrate this simple explanation of the theory of vowels and not with any intention of supplying shapes and positions for the student to imitate. From the diagram it will be noticed that the vowel quality depends upon tongue *and* lip positions, and the previous paragraph must not be misconstrued in which it was stated that "Some vowels depend mainly upon the tongue, others depend much upon the lips".

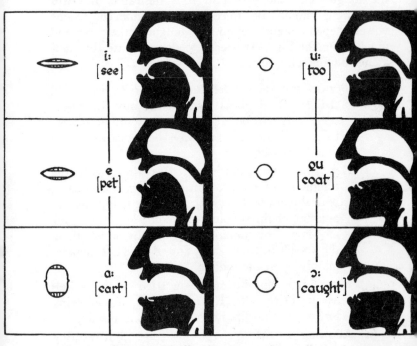

Fig. 1.—Diagrams indicating approximate lip and tongue positions for the vowels in SEE, PET, CART, TOO, COAT, CAUGHT.

In this chapter it is intended to consider the vowel sounds generally used in English speech, lists of which will be given. The symbols used are intended to supply an introduction to writing and reading in phonetic script, an ability by no means indispensable to the acquirement of good speech, but a qualification frequently, and wisely, required by various examining bodies. One of the uses of a good phonetic script (a script in which each sound has a separate symbol) may be recognised by the difficulty of indicating the forty or so sounds used in English by an alphabet containing only twenty-six symbols. The futility of attempting to rely upon our ordinary alphabet will be fully appreciated when the student realises that in our normal spelling the *one letter* "A" has, for example, to represent *six* different vowel *sounds* in "B*a*th *a*ll the b*a*re bl*a*ck b*a*bies *a*gain".

A SIMPLE or PURE VOWEL is unchanged during its utterance, and in Standard Received English there are twelve such vowels:

The SIMPLE Vowel in—	Represented by the PHONETIC SYMBOL :	The key-word written phonetically :
s*ee*	iː	siː
l*i*p	i	lip
t*e*n	e	ten
b*a*ck	æ	bæk
gl*a*ss	ɑː	glɑːs
n*o*t	ɔ	nɔt
sm*a*ll	ɔː	smɔːl
b*oo*k	u	buk
tw*o*	uː	tuː
*u*p	ʌ	ʌp
b*i*rd	əː	bəːd
*a*bove	ə	əbʌv

A special note is required about the vowel ə, known as the NEUTRAL VOWEL. It is the commonest vowel in English speech, and occurs in almost all unstressed syllables in place of the vowel which would be used in the stressed form of the same syllable. Compare the

B

"natural" pronunciations of the word "and" in the following examples:

> Bread and butter.
> Not once did he use the word "and".

It will have been noticed that in the first example the pronunciation was ənd, and in the second it was ænd. This neutralising of vowels in their unstressed forms is of great importance in connection with the question of emphasis and also in regard to speech rhythm, both of which matters will be dealt with later.

A DIPHTHONG or DOUBLE VOWEL is formed by joining two simple vowels as, for example, joining e and i to form the vowel as in "plate", which would be transcribed phonetically as pleit. The following nine diphthongs are recognised:

The DIPHTHONG in—	Represented by the PHONETIC SYMBOL:	The key-word written phonetically:
plate	ei	pleit
go	ou	gou
knife	ai	naif
count	au	kaunt
boy	ɔi	bɔi
ear	iə	iə
wear	ɛə	wɛə
more	ɔə	mɔə
poor	uə	puə

It is of practical importance in the pronunciation of diphthongs that each of the pure sounds shall be accurately formed. The cockney form of "night" is often the result

VOWELS 19

of combining ɔː and iː instead of a and i. In some
Northern variants the second sound of the diphthong is
frequently dropped altogether as in soːp instead of soup
(used for washing, not for drinking) and keːk instead of
keik for "cake".

The correct formation of vowels is most satisfactorily
achieved by the imitation of good examples. The
standard sounds, having been aurally recognised and
faithfully reproduced, must be mentally registered and
used in exercises and in normal speech until the right
habits are formed, and until the initial period of self-
consciousness has passed into the "natural" use of the
newly acquired sound.

It is possible to kill two birds with one stone by beginning
to read exercises in phonetic script, practising the vowels
and at the same time becoming familiar with the symbols.
The scope of the exercises must of necessity be very limited
until the consonant symbols have been learnt, but the
following will suffice, having been arranged to contain
only those consonants which are pronounced in a way
familiarly associated with a common symbol:

iː	wiː niːd tu siː əbaut fiftiːn ɔː sikstiːn fiːt	We need to see about fifteen or sixteen feet.
i	sidni kwikli likt hiz lips	Sidney quickly licked his lips.
e	send twenti pɛəz tu: evri ten men	Send twenty pairs to every ten men.
æ	ə blæk mæn brɔːt bæk auə sæk	A black man brought back our sack.
ɑː	mai klɑːs ɑːskt tu gou tu klɑːktaun	My class asked to go to Clarktown.
ɔ	mai beibiz kɔt wəz nɔt ɔn tɔmz lɔri	My baby's cot was not on Tom's lorry.

ɔː	pɔːl ɔːt tu ɔːdə səm mɔə bɔːlz fə hiz kɔːts	Paul ought to order some more balls for his courts.
u	auə dɔktə tuk ə luk ət mai fut	Our doctor took a look at my foot.
uː	pliːz duː nɔt huːt tuː suːn	Please do not hoot too soon.
ʌ	if wiː aː lʌki sʌm mʌni wil kʌm	If we are lucky some money will come.
əː	pəːsi bəːnt bəːts kəːtnz	Percy burnt Bert's curtains.
ei	treinz mei biː leit tudei	Trains may be late to-day.
ou	hiː gouz houm tu roum bai bout	He goes home to Rome by boat.
ai	mai hait is faiv fut nain	My height is five foot nine.
au	hau əbaut ə raund braun kraun	How about a round brown crown?
ɔi	it bɔild ənd bɔild ʌntil it wəz spɔild	It boiled and boiled until it was spoiled.
iə	mistə wiə did nɔt fiər auə wiər ʌntil it wəz niə	Mr Weir did not fear our weir until it was near.
ɛə	mɛəri did nɔt kɛə tu gou tu bænbəri fɛə	Mary did not care to go to Banbury Fair.
ɔə	mɔə drɔəz in auə stɔəz niːd tu biː bɔəd	More drawers in our stores need to be bored.
uə	fjuə puə wud biː kjuəd	Fewer poor would be cured.

There are good reasons why a more detailed study of vowels is considered to be necessary. The first of these reasons is that a sound background knowledge of the mechanics of language might at any time supply the right answer to a practical professional problem, and the second reason is due to the fact that there are to be found, but fortunately only occasionally, students of insensitive aural perception who, in consequence, find it impossible to produce the correct sound "by ear". Such students might well be assisted by the more mechanical method of studying and applying the analytical data of the sound under treatment. It must be emphasised, however, that there is general agreement among the specialists that this "mouth-positioning" method should never be used until it has been definitely established that the "aural-imitative" method is impracticable. To serve these purposes it is not necessary to analyse speech sounds as exhaustively as would be required for a serious study of phonetics. The object of this book will be well served if vowels are classified as follows:

1. BY THE HEIGHT OF THE TONGUE. In some vowels the tongue has a high position, allowing only a narrow passage for the vowel. Such vowels, referred to as "*Close*" (or "High") vowels, are—

	iː	i	uː		u
as in	peep	pip	through	and	look

To produce other vowels the tongue is low and tending to flatness. The air passage is correspondingly well open. These "*Open*" (or "Low") vowels are—

	ɑː		ʌ
as in	path	and	luck

As a simple experiment, examine with a mirror the formation of these vowels, and it will be observed that in the formation of the "Open" vowels the view of the throat is not obstructed.

Between these two extreme classes there is the "*Semi-close*" vowel:

as in

e

let

and the "*Semi-open*" vowels:

	æ	ɔ	ɔː	əː		ə
as in	back	cot	caught	purse	and	about

(the first neutral syllable in the last example).

Fig. 1 also indicates the difference of tongue position between uː, a close vowel, and ɑː, an open vowel.

2. As to whether the Front or the Back of the Tongue is used. For some vowels the front of the tongue is bunched up, and for others the back of the tongue is bunched up. The former are called "*Front*" vowels:

	iː	i	e		æ
as in	heed	hid	peck	and	lack

and the latter are called "*Back*" vowels:

	uː	u	ɔː	ɔ		ɑː
as in	brood	put	born	doll	and	cart

When the middle of the tongue is bunched up, the result is what is called a "*Mixed*" vowel, of which there are three:

ʌ   əː   ə

as in cut learnt and (the first neutral syllable in) above.

Again, the diagrams (Fig. 1) illustrate the tongue in "Front" position for e, and in "Back" position for ɑː.

The accuracy of vowels in English depends very much on the tongue being positioned as stated above, the result of which is virtually to divide the mouth and the pharynx into two resonators in series, instead of allowing these cavities to form one long resonator as would be the case with the tongue completely flat and inactive. It is the combination of the two distinctly different frequencies thus produced (one behind and one in front of the tongue "hump") which results in the characteristic sound associated with a particular vowel position.

3. POSITION OF THE LIPS. As has been previously stated, however, the lips are also important, not only for actual "shaping" of the vowel quality, but also in "rounding the tone". The lips have been likened to the bell of a wind instrument, which is known to affect the musical quality greatly. Generally speaking, the lips are rounded and protruded for,

u: and ɔ:

as in   food and ford

the orifice increasing in size for the latter.

For the formation of—

i: i   e

as in   creed fin and pence

the lips are in a spread position.

The remaining vowels require a lip position consistent with the degree of jaw movement necessitated by the tongue position.

4. LENGTH OR DURATION. In the phonetic symbols introduced in this chapter the (:) symbol is a sign of length or duration of the vowel and is used to indicate that—

i: ɑ: ɔ: u: ɜ:

as in   seek farm pork fool and skirt

are "*Long*" vowels. The remainder being known as "*Short*".

5. PURE OR DIPHTHONGAL. It has already been explained that diphthongs are the result of rapidly moving from one pure vowel to another. The phonetic symbols

clearly show which two pure vowels form the component parts of the recognised diphthongs:

ei ou ai au ɔi iə ɛə ɔə uə
as in pain hope life crowd boy fear where four sure.

In three of these diphthongs the initial sound is not included in the list of pure vowels because they never occur alone as pure vowels; they occur only when combined with another vowel to form a diphthong. These three sounds are—

ɛ a o

and are the initial sounds in the diphthongs in the words, *care*, *sound* and *hope* respectively.

Exercises for Vowels fall into two distinct divisions, according as to whether their purpose is (*a*) to develop the necessary flexibility of the speech organs to allow them to respond quickly in forming accurately the sounds required, or (*b*) to practise the accurate formation of sounds, diagnosed as faulty, until correct formation becomes habitual.

The following *exercises* are suggested for FLEXIBILITY OF JAW, TONGUE AND LIPS for vowel formation:

1. Jaw. Begin by observing the difference between "opening the mouth" and "dropping the jaw". The former is usually a muscularly rigid action; the latter should be conceived as the falling of the lower jaw-bone by *releasing the tension of the muscles* which normally hold it up. Exercises should consist of—

(*a*) allowing the jaw to drop, released, to its limit, and
(*b*) quickly repeated lateral movements of the jaw while it "hangs loosely down". Then
(*c*) with jaw still down, protrude it forward and draw it back, repeating this also in quick succession.

2. TONGUE. With mouth loosely open (teeth separated by about 1 inch) say or sing—

ɔː lɑː lɔː lɑː . . . . . . lɔː lɑː
(law lah law lah . . . . . . law lah),

observing the following points. The jaw should not move during the exercise. It must remain relaxed and easily open while the activity is confined to the tongue, which should work quite independently. There should be a sensation of the tongue "falling" to the floor of the mouth for the vowels, with its tip in contact with the back surfaces of the lower front teeth.

3. LIPS. Move the lips in quick repetition as if to speak,

iː ɔː iː ɔː iː ɔː . . . . . . iː ɔː
(ee aw ee aw ee aw . . . . . . ee aw),

but without phonating the vowels. Keep the exercise as silent lip movements, but elongate and pout the lips alternately as if you wished to exaggerate the pronunciation of the vowels.

EXERCISES FOR VOWEL PRACTICE

1. Repeated imitation from standard examples of the sounds under treatment.

2. Exercises from lists of isolated words containing the required vowel sounds.

3. Speaking sentences, in which the sound is repeated, with fluent speech rhythm. These sentences should be invented by the student along the lines of those given on pages 19 and 20.

N.B.—Every effort should be made to correct faulty sounds "by ear". Only when this method fails should use be made of instructions derived from the analytical facts given in this chapter.

PHONETIC SCRIPT. Not all students will be interested in the use of phonetic script, and, therefore, throughout the whole of this and the next chapter, transcriptions are given side by side with the ordinary printed form. For practical purposes it will make little difference whether the phonetic symbols are used or not. For students who are interested it is suggested—

1. Cover the right-hand half of pages 19 and 20 and read the sentences from the phonetic script, checking, when necessary, from the "key".

2. Cover the left-hand half of the text and write out the sentences in phonetic script, correcting your attempts afterwards by comparison with the transcription given.

CHAPTER 3

CONSONANTS

Consonants are caused by the complete or partial stoppage of voice or breath by the organs of articulation, which are the tongue, teeth, lips, hard and soft palates, and, in the case of the "h" sound, the vocal cords. Whilst vowels, in the main, give colour, consonants, as it were, supply the outline to the picture of our speech. In general, they connect one vowel to another (*L. articulus,* a joint). Vowels are used largely for the production of adequate vocal tone, whilst the consonants are used to give distinctness to speech. Thus volume can best be developed in connection with vowels, and distinct speech is best achieved by firmly controlled activity and accurately co-ordinated contacts of the articulatory organs.

The student has already been warned against becoming too much concerned with conscious "mouth-shaping" of vowels; he was advised to rely mainly upon his ear. With regard to consonants, however, it is often possible to correct or improve articulation by explaining the nature and place of the contacts required, in practice its being found much easier consciously to make a definite tongue movement than to hold a definite tongue position. Making a tongue movement does not usually result in rigidity; attempting to hold a tongue position frequently does, and any form of rigidity is the worst possible enemy of the speaker. It is of practical importance to emphasise this difference of approach between vowels and consonants. Teaching vowels by "diagram-imitation" frequently leads to some form of tension, and the concentration being on the physical cause rather than on the oral result, aural sensitivity is not sufficiently relied upon, and this method should be used only as a last resort. Teaching consonants should also be attempted "by ear", but, if necessitated by circumstances, diagrams, explanations and physical descriptions may be used with less risk of muscular rigidity being caused.

In examining the following list of consonants used in English, the student must guard against the common mistake of confusing sounds with the letters which represent them in the ordinary alphabet. For example, the letter "B" (pronounced biː) contains a consonant and a vowel, b and iː respectively. Similarly juː (the pronunciation of the letter "U") is the consonant j followed by the vowel uː.

The CONSONANT SOUND in—	Represented by the PHONETIC SYMBOL:	The key-word written phonetically:
*p*et	p	pet
*b*at	b	bæt
*t*in	t	tin
*d*eed	d	diːd
*k*ind	k	kaind
*g*ood	g	gud
*m*en	m	men
*n*ew	n	njuː
ki*ng*	ŋ	kiŋ
*l*oot	l	luːt
wa*ll*	ł	wɔːł
*w*ill	w	wil
*wh*en	ʍ	ʍen (or hwen)
*f*ull	f	ful
*v*ery	v	veri
*th*ose	ð	ðouz
*th*ink	θ	θiŋk
*s*ix	s	siks
*z*ebra	z	ziːbrə
a*r*ound	r	əraund

THE CONSONANT SOUND in—	Represented by the PHONETIC SYMBOL:	The key-word written phonetically:
*sh*ut	ʃ	ʃʌt
plea*s*ure	ʒ	pleʒə
*h*is	h	hiz
*ch*in	tʃ	tʃin
*j*oke	dʒ	dʒouk
*y*ear	j	jiə

In the formation of English consonants the necessary obstructions are caused by contacts at seven points which may be clearly identified.

Obstruction Point and organs used.	Technical description.	Consonants produced.					
Lip—lip	bilabial	p	b	m	w	ʍ	
Teeth—lip	labio-dental	f	v				
Teeth—blade of tongue	linguo dental	θ	ð				
Teeth ridge—blade of tongue	alveolar	t	d	n	r	s	z
		ʃ	ʒ	l	ł	tʃ	dʒ
Hard palate—front of tongue	palatal	j					
Soft palate—back of tongue	velar	k	g	ŋ	w		
Vocal cords	glottal	h	ʍ				

Notice that w and ʍ are formed by two simultaneous obstructions. In each case there is a front obstruction caused by the rounding of the lips to form a small orifice, in addition to which there is a back obstruction, between the soft palate and the back of the tongue for the w, and between the vocal cords for the ʍ.

The above classification is made clear by the diagram in Fig. 2 from which the various parts of the tongue should be noted.

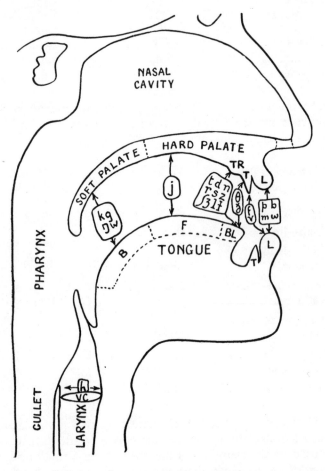

FIG. 2.—Sectional diagram, showing points of contact for the articulation of the consonants. TR, teeth ridge. T, teeth. L, lip. B, back, F, front, and BL, blade of tongue. VC, vocal cords.

From a simple observation of the two consonants p and f another important classification will be recognised. The sound p is representative of a complete obstruction and f of an incomplete obstruction. In the former example the exit is momentarily completely closed during which the breath is compressed, and is allowed to escape almost immediately by the sudden removal of the obstruction. In the latter example, the obstruction is not complete, but the articulatory organs (in this case the lower lip and the upper teeth) are brought into an imperfect contact which "squeezes" the breath, causing the sound (f) by friction.

Sounds caused by *complete obstruction* of both nose and mouth are called PLOSIVES, and are represented by the symbols:

b p d t g k

In the formation of other consonants the term "complete obstruction" refers to mouth obstruction only, the voice being allowed to escape through the nose; these are called NASALS, represented by—

m n ŋ

The principal subdivisions of the *incomplete obstructions* are FRICATIVES, caused by escaping breath or voice, of which some are known as SIMPLE FRICATIVES:

f v θ ð r h

and others as SIBILANT FRICATIVES, by reason of their shrillness; these are:

s z ʃ ʒ

Lastly, under the general term "Fricative" is the "LATERAL" type of consonant:

l ɫ

so called because the sound passes round the sides of the tongue, the blade of which is in firm contact with the teeth ridge.

SEMI-VOWELS are consonant forms of vowels. In English there are two such sounds:

w and j

the former related to the vowel u, and the latter related to the vowel i.

An AFFRICATE is a combination of a plosive and a fricative. In English there are two such sounds:

tʃ and dʒ

The student will find by experiment that by combining the first sound of "take" with the first sound of "shut" he can produce the first sound of "chunk". This could have been said very much more economically by using the phonetic symbols: $t + ʃ = tʃ$, which is also a much more scientific way of writing the explanation. Similarly $d + ʒ = dʒ$ (as in *judge*).

A last, and very useful, way in which consonants may be classified depends upon the fact that some sounds are emitted as "breath-sounds" only, whilst others are "vocalised". A simple test of the two sounds, b and p, will easily determine that voice is used in making the b. If you feel your throat very lightly between thumb and finger, you will feel a vibration of the vocal cords when making the b sound, which you do not feel when making the p sound which requires breath only. Sounds requiring voice are referred to as VOICED (or vocal), and sounds requiring breath only are said to be VOICELESS (or unvoiced or aspirate).

The following list shows the voiced consonants tabulated with the corresponding unvoiced consonants. There are a number of deficiences among the voiceless and one deficiency in the voiced consonants. It is possible to make all the articulations voiced or unvoiced, but there are phonetic reasons why this has not been developed.

That there are about twice the number of voiced compared with the unvoiced in English is no doubt due to

the fact that unvoiced sounds do not carry well, while many
of the voiced consonants have a fine musical quality,
several of them being more musical than certain vowels.

The following list completes the various bases of
classification:

VOICED Consonants	VOICELESS Consonants	VOICED Consonants	VOICELESS Consonants
b	p	r	–
d	t	j	–
g	k	–	h
m	–	z	s
n	–	ʒ	ʃ
ŋ	–	l	–
w	ʍ	ɫ	–
v	f	dʒ	tʃ
ð	θ		

When a faulty consonant is detected, and when
attempted imitation of a correct example has been found
to be ineffective, the above classifications can be used
with much advantage in the analysis of the fault or faults.
Answers to one or more of the following questions will
show where the fault lies:

(*a*) What place of obstruction is supposed to result in
the consonant under examination?

(*b*) Should the obstruction be (1) complete, or (2)
incomplete?

(*c*) If the answer to (*b*) is (1), should the sound be
plosive or nasal? If the answer to (*b*) is (2),
should the sound be a simple or a sibilant
fricative or a lateral?

(*d*) If the sound is classifiable as an affricate, then are
the two sounds of which it is composed both
correct in their formation?

(*e*) Should the sound be vocalised or only aspirated?

A comparison between detailed answers to the above and the activity responsible for the faulty consonant will usually show clearly the specific error and will give a scientific indication of the necessary correction.

A complete list of consonants, with practice sentences, is given below, and if treated as the corresponding vowel exercise was treated in the previous chapter, it will assist in consonant exercises and also in the recognition of their symbols. The student will have noticed that in this chapter fewer key-words have been used. It is expected that he will by now have become sufficiently familiar with the idea of writing in phonetic script, and in the following exercises it has been thought advisable to add "Accent" marks to indicate the stressed syllables.

p	pliːz aːsk ˈpiːtəsən | ðə ˈplɑːstərə ˈpeintər ənd ˈpeipə'hæŋə | tə ˈpəːtʃəs piŋk ˈpeipə fə pæts ruːm |	Please ask Peterson, the plasterer, painter and paper-hanger, to purchase pink paper for Pat's room.
b	biɫ ˈbaundəd biˈhaind ðə ˈbiɫstənz bɑːn | tə ˈbɔrou bəːts ˈbaisikl |	Bill bounded behind the Bilstons' barn to borrow Bert's bicycle.
t	ˈtjuːzdi wiɫ biː tuː leit | tə tɔːk tə ðə ˈtiːtʃəz | əbaut ðə ˈteiɫə ˈtɔmsən riˈpɔːt |	Tuesday will be too late to talk to the teachers about the Taylor-Thompson report.
d	ðə ˈdɔŋkæstə ˈdentists diˈsaidəd | nɔt tə diˈvʌldʒ ðə deit | tə ðə ˈdərektər əv ðə ˈdentistri də ˈpɑːtmənt |	The Doncaster dentists decided not to divulge the date to the director of the dentistry department.
k	ðə kiŋks ənd kəːɫz əv ˈkeiti ˈkəːbiz ˈklʌstriŋ hɛə | kɔːzd kiːn ˈkɔment |	The kinks and curls of Katie Curby's clustering hair caused keen comment.

g	gud 'greiʃəs | kraid 'gregəri | əz ðə greit goust ground 'guːliʃli | ənd 'gəːgld 'gruːsəmli |	"Good gracious!" cried Gregory, as the great ghost groaned ghoulishly, and gurgled gruesomely.
m	'mɔdən 'mjuːzik meiks 'meni men mæd wið 'meɫənkɔɫi |	Modern music makes many men mad with melancholy.
n	ðə 'njuːmrəs 'njuːsənsəz ni'sesiteitəd ə 'nʌmbər əv njuː lɔːz |	The numerous nuisances necessitated a number of new laws.
ŋ	'djuəriŋ ðə 'mɔːniŋz | ənd ɔn lɔŋ 'liŋgəriŋ 'iːvniŋz | wi kud hiə ðəm 'pleiiŋ | siŋiŋ ənd 'daːnsiŋ | 'seɫdəm 'restiŋ ɔː 'sliːpiŋ |	During the mornings and on long lingering evenings, we could hear them playing, singing and dancing, seldom resting or sleeping.
l and ɫ	'loumæks 'liŋgəd lɔŋ ənd 'lʌviŋli | ʍen kəm'peɫd tə teik hiz 'fɛəwel frəm ðə 'lʌvli gleidz | ənd tə ri'təːn tə 'livə'puːɫ |	Lomax lingered long and lovingly, when compelled to take his farewell from the lovely glades and to return to Liverpool.
w and ʍ	ʍaiɫ 'wiɫjəm 'wʌndəd ʍeðə hiː wəz 'mɔːtəli 'wuːndəd | ðə 'kwestʃənz əv ʍiðə hiː ʃud biː sent | ənd frəm ʍens həd hiː kʌm | bi'wiɫdəd hiz 'waiɫi 'kæptəz |	While William wondered whether he was mortally wounded, the questions of whither he should be sent and from whence had he come, bewildered his wily captors.
f	faiv 'hʌndrəd ənd 'fifti faiv 'frentʃmən fɔːt 'fiəsli ə'geinst ə fə'rouʃəs fou |	Five hundred and fifty-five Frenchmen fought fiercely against a ferocious foe.

v   ðə və'lju:minəs roubz əv 'velvət wə 'veri ə'træktiv | ʌen lə'viniə wəz 'vestəd |

The voluminous robes of velvet were very attractive when Lavinia was vested.

ð   ðə 'θiəriz əv ðouz deiz |
and   nɔtwi ð'stændiŋ ðə' θauzəndz əv paundz spent
θ   ən ðəm | wə nɔt 'θʌrəli θɔːt aut | ənd 'meni 'θauzəndz əv ðə 'piːpl 'periʃt θruː nou fɔːlt əv ðɛər oun |

The theories of those days, notwithstanding the thousands of pounds spent on them, were not thoroughly thought out, and many thousands of the people perished through no fault of their own.

s   ðə 'soułdjəz wə sent tə
and   sik'juə ðə siks 'ziːbrəz
z   ʌitʃ həd əs'keipt frəm ðə 'sentrəl zuː | ənd huːz 'eskəpeidz həd 'dzepədaizd ðə 'seifti əv ðə 'sitizənz |

The soldiers were sent to secure the six zebras which had escaped from the central zoo, and whose escapades had jeopardised the safety of the citizens.

r   ðə ri'łentləs 'strʌglz əv ðə kruː'seidəz 'djuəriŋ ðə 'revə'łjuːʃən pri'ventəd ə greit diəł əv 'retʃədnəs |

The relentless struggles of the crusaders during the revolution prevented a great deal of wretchedness.

ʃ   'ʃuəłi ðə ʃugə seiłz ʃud ʃou səm 'prɔfit bifɔː wiː ʃʌt daun |

Surely the sugar sales should show some profit before we shut down.

ʒ   it wəz ə 'pleʒə | 'djuəriŋ auər ə'keiʒənəl leʒə | tu en'dʒɔi ðiː 'eiʒuə skai | ənd tə 'treʒə ðə 'viʒənz tə bi rə'membəd 'leitə |

It was a pleasure during our occasional leisure to enjoy the azure sky and to treasure the visions to be remembered later.

h	hiː 'hʌrid ɑːftə 'hæri | 'houpiŋ tə hiə ðət hiz hænd həd hiːɫd |	He hurried after Harry, hoping to hear that his hand had healed.
tʃ	ɔːɫ'ðou tʃɑːɫz wəz ə tʃiːt | hiː wəz tʃɑːmiŋ ‖ hiː wəz nɔt ə gud tʃes 'pleiə ‖ hiː pri'fɔːd tə tʌtʃ hiz frendz fər ən ə'keiʒənəl tʃek |	Although Charles was a cheat, he was charming. He was not a good chess player. He preferred to "touch" his friends for an occasional cheque.
dʒ	ðə peidʒ hæd tə dʒʌdʒ frəm ðə 'kʌɫə(r)əv ðə lɑːdʒ dʒem | əz tə 'ʍeðə sɔː dʒɔːdʒ həd biːn 'dʒoukiŋ |	The page had to judge from the colour of the large gem as to whether Sir George had been joking.
j	jet hiː njuː ðət if juː wəː tə stei wið ðə djuːk fər ə jiər in jɔːk | juː wud nɔt faind hiz hjuːdʒ haus 'veri 'sjuːtəbl |	Yet he knew that if you were to stay with the Duke for a year in York, you would not find his huge house very suitable.

By practising the sentences given above, and by correcting any articulatory faults along the lines suggested on page 33, the student should try to acquire a clear, but easy and unforced, style of speech before passing on to the next stage which deals with the technique of vocal expression. Otherwise he will find it difficult to concentrate on expressiveness if he has constantly to be reminded of mechanical weaknesses in his speech formation.

1. EXERCISES FOR FLEXIBILITY OF TONGUE
   (a) Produce a sustained trilled r but without voice—that is, an aspirated trilled r.
   (b) Repeat t t t t t t . . . . . t t.
   (c) Repeat d d d d d . . . . . . d d.
   (d) Similarly with any sounds needing special exercise.

2. EXERCISES FOR FLEXIBILITY OF THE LIPS

    (*a*) Produce loose vibration of lips, sustaining it as long as breath permits.

    (*b*) Repeat b b b b b . . . . . . b b.

    (*c*) Repeat p p p p p . . . . . . p p.

3. PHONETIC SCRIPT

    Students interested in phonetic transcription should work through the exercises on pages 34–37, adapting the instructions given for the vowel exercises on page 26.

4. REVISION

    Read through this and the previous chapter, repeating conscientiously all the exercises before proceeding.

CHAPTER 4

VOCAL EXPRESSION

The mechanism of speech, outlined in the previous chapters, should form the basis of habits, at first consciously adopted and afterwards unconsciously applied in natural everyday usage. As to how quickly new speech habits can be consolidated depends upon many factors, such as age, environment, stimulus of professional necessity and so on. The mechanical side, however, must not be laboured. The student should learn the essentials as efficiently as possible, and he should, by frequent revision, endeavour to embody them in his normal form of address. But the process takes time, and the most fatal mistake is to prolong a concentrated study of the mechanics, resulting in a technical attitude rather than an imaginative approach.

The only sound attitude towards speech-training is that which focuses attention constantly upon expressiveness, vitality and spontaneity of utterance. Therefore, as soon as it becomes permissible, the student should devote less attention to speech formation, and develop an ever-increasing concentration upon any device by which vocal expression may be made more vigorous.

Among the various factors by which meaning is expressed, first place must be given to PHRASING. In the nomenclature of speech-training, the definition of the word "phrase" is not necessarily the same as that used by the grammarian whose primary concern is with the writing of literary English. For purposes of oral expression, a phrase is best defined as "a group of words expressing a mental concept", and this "sense-unit" is spoken for convenience on one breath-impulse, although it is not generally necessary, in fact it would be distracting, to replenish the breath between every phrase. Punctuation is indicated by PAUSE.

The procedure involved may seem somewhat complicated to explain, but it can be managed quite unobtrusively if fully understood at the outset by analysing a short exercise. This analysis also serves to introduce the relation of speaker to listener. The sentence is divided into phrases as indicated:

A,C,   a,b, B,C,
　　"The maid of the house/with her face upon her
　　　　　　a,b, B,C,   a,b, B,C,
　　folded arms/more audibly expressed her grief/than
　　　　　　　　a,b,
　　any of the others."

What actually takes place when the sentence is clearly spoken may best be explained as follows:

SPEAKER. A. The speaker conceives the sentence generally, and the first phrase specifically, and unconsciously inhales breath in anticipation of speaking.

B. The speaker conceives the next phrase; breath is inhaled if necessary.

C. The phrase is spoken on one breath-impulse.

LISTENER. a. The listener hears the phrase.

b. The listener has time to register the import of the phrase.

Each phrase thus communicates the minimum sense-unit, and the meaning, previously broken-down by the speaker, is rebuilt into a whole in the mind of the listener.

Probably the commonest fault is the failure to keep each phrase down to a single mental concept. Self-discipline is necessary and will be repaid by coherent expression.

Especially should the student guard against being misled by the punctuation of the written word, generally intended to be read silently and requiring a mental rather than a physical effort. The grammatical punctuation should be accepted as a guide to make clear the sense to the student as a "reader". As a "speaker" he must make many modifications, and in general must add many pauses to those indicated by the full stops, commas and other marks of punctuation.

Sentences generally contain several phrases. The phrases comprise the sentence, just as the sentences make up an entire paragraph, and the paragraphs build up into the chapter. At the end of the sentence, the listener quite naturally requires a little more time to assimilate the meaning of the sentence than that which he requires for each phrase of which the sentence is composed. The pause at the end of the sentence should, therefore, be of rather longer duration than the pause after each phrase. These pauses are known as SENSE PAUSES. Quite manifestly they are determined by meaning.

The following exercise is especially useful as it shows that many more pauses are necessary than those indicated by the grammatical punctuation. In regard, generally, to the following exercises, the student should do his best with each selection for the purpose for which it is set. He should add the relevant parts of technique as they are dealt with. Even when attempting verse excerpts, he should not at present concern himself with metre nor with the technique of verse-speaking.

I am always very well pleased with a country Sunday;/ and think,/if keeping holy the seventh day/were only a human institution,/it would be the best method/that could have been thought of/for the polishing/and civilising/of mankind. It is certain the country people would soon degenerate into a kind of savages and barbarians, were there not such frequent returns of a stated time, in which

the whole village meet together with their best faces, and
in their cleanliest habits, to converse with one another upon
indifferent subjects, hear their duties explained to them, and
join together in adoration of the Supreme Being. Sunday
clears away the rust of the whole week, not only as it
refreshes in their minds the notions of religion, but as it
puts both the sexes upon appearing in their most agreeable
forms, and exerting all such qualities as are apt to give them
a figure in the eye of the village. A country fellow dis-
tinguishes himself as much in the churchyard as a citizen
does upon the Change, the whole parish politics being
generally discussed in that place either after sermon or
before the bell rings.

My friend Sir Roger, being a good churchman, has
beautified the inside of his church with several texts of his
own choosing: he has likewise given a handsome pulpit-
cloth, and railed in the communion-table at his own
expense. He has often told me, that at his coming to his
estate, he found his parishioners very irregular; and that
in order to make them kneel and join in the responses, he
gave every one of them a hassoc and a Common Prayer
Book; and at the same time employed an itinerant singing-
master, who goes about the country for that purpose, to
instruct them rightly in the tunes of the psalms; upon
which they now very much value themselves, and indeed
out-do most of the country churches that I have ever
heard.

As Sir Roger is landlord to the whole congregation, he
keeps them in very good order, and will suffer nobody to
sleep in it besides himself; for if by chance he has been
surprised into a short nap at sermon, upon recovering out
of it he stands up and looks about him, and if he sees anybody else nodding, either wakes them himself, or sends his
servant to them. Several other of the old knight's par-
ticularities break out upon these occasions: sometimes he
will be lengthening out a verse in the singing-psalms, half
a minute after the rest of the congregation have done with
it; sometimes, when he is pleased with the matter of his
devotion, he pronounces Amen three or four times to the

same prayer; and sometimes stands up when everybody else is upon their knees, to count the congregation, or see if any of his tenants are missing.

I was yesterday very much surprised to hear my old friend in the midst of the service, calling out to one John Matthews to mind what he was about, and not disturb the congregation. This John Matthews, it seems, is remarkable for being an idle fellow, and at that time was kicking his heels for his diversion. This authority of the knight, though exerted in that odd manner which accompanies him in all circumstances of life, has a very good effect upon the parish, who are not polite enough to see anything ridiculous in his behaviour; besides that the general good sense and worthiness of his character, make his friends observe these little singularities as foils that rather set off than blemish his good qualities.

As soon as the sermon is finished, nobody presumes to stir till Sir Roger is gone out of the church. The knight walks down from his seat in the chancel between a double row of his tenants, that stand bowing to him on each side; and every now and then he inquires how such an one's wife, or mother, or son, or father do, whom he does not see at church; which is understood as a secret reprimand to the person that is absent.

The chaplain has often told me, that upon a catechising-day, when Sir Roger has been pleased with a boy that answers well, he has ordered a Bible to be given him next day for his encouragement; and sometimes accompanies it with a flitch of bacon to his mother. Sir Roger has likewise added five pounds a year to the clerk's place; and that he may encourage the young fellows to make themselves perfect in the church-service, has promised, upon the death of the present incumbent, who is very old, to bestow it according to merit.

The fair understanding between Sir Roger and his chaplain, and their mutual concurrence in doing good, is the more remarkable, because the very next village is famous for the difference and contentions that arise between the parson and the 'squire, and the 'squire, to be revenged on

the parson, never comes to church. The 'squire has made
all his tenants atheists and tithe-stealers; while the parson
instructs them every Sunday in the dignity of his order, and
insinuates to them, almost in every sermon, that he is a
better man than his patron. In short, matters are come to
such an extremity, that the 'squire has not said his prayers
either in public or private this half year; and that the
parson threatens him, if he does not mend his manners, to
pray for him in the face of the whole congregation.

Feuds of this nature, though too frequent in the country,
are very fatal to the ordinary people; who are so used to be
dazzled with riches, that they pay as much deference to the
understanding of a man of an estate, as of a man of learning;
and are very hardly brought to regard any truth, how
important soever it may be, that is preached to them, when
they know there are several men of five hundred a year who
do not believe it.

ADDISON, *Spectator*, No. 112.

Having mentioned the matter of PAUSE, it might be as
well to outline the classification of pauses into three groups.
Firstly, pauses which depend on sense. As already
explained, these depend upon the speaker's grasp of the
meaning, and they are used in order that communication
may be clear. Such pauses have already been labelled
as sense pauses.

The next group is of pauses which depend upon emotion
and imagination, the position and duration of which are
entirely a matter of feeling. The following examples
will suffice for the present.

O, pardon me, thou bleeding piece of earth,
That I am meek and gentle with these ⌒ butchers!
Julius Cæsar, III, 1.

And Nathan said to David, ⌒ Thou ⌒ art the man.
2 Samuel, xii, 7.

Various descriptions have been given to the pauses of
this group—emotional, oratorical, rhetorical, dramatic

and the like—so many as to be confusing. They are perhaps best described as EMOTIONAL PAUSES. Quite clearly they are dependent upon feeling rather than upon sense. It is essential, however, that the word "emotion" shall not be so interpreted as to result in theatrical or stagey mannerisms.

The third group contains those pauses necessitated by the rhythmic factor in speech and are associated with verse-speaking. These will be the subject of later discussion in connection with the interpretation and rendering of verse forms.

Different as these various kinds of pauses are in purpose and application, there is one rule, common to them all, which cannot be over-emphasised. A pause must never interrupt the continuity of a speech. Temporary vocal cessation there must be, but mental continuity must be carried through the pause, so that atmosphere is sustained.

It is quite clear that varying degrees of power are used in the different syllables of a word, the different words in a phrase, and, indeed, the different phrases of a sentence. It is these gradations of power, resulting from variations either of volume or of intensity, which indicate the relative importance of some words and phrases in comparison with others.

Pronunciation depends almost as much upon the speaker placing the ACCENT on the correct syllable as upon using intelligible speech sounds. It is the position of the accent which changes the words "desert" and "record" from verbs to nouns. There is nothing reasonable about the pronunciation of English, and the dictionary should be consulted in case of doubt. At the same time it should be remembered that pronunciation is constantly changing and the student must try to ascertain the correct pronunciation of the words for the period from which a selection or play might be chosen. For example, in Shakespeare's time the accent was on the second syllable of "conjure", and in a later period "theatre" was accented on the second syllable. Unless such care is taken, especially in the speaking of verse, the rhythmic flow intended by the writer will be spoilt. Naturally this advice does not apply to Early or Middle English which has already been translated into Modern English.

Because of its association with rhythm, syllabic accent is of great importance in connection with fluency. The position of the accents control, unconsciously, the arrangement of the words in order to produce the smoothest rhythmic flow. In the following very obvious example, the changing of the word-order is responsible for completely upsetting the rhythm.

"Over the cobbles he clattered and clashed. . . ."
He clashed and clattered over the cobbles.

Rhythmic flow is generally associated with the speaking of verse, but prose has its own rhythm, not restricted by a metrical formula, but none the less essential to smooth fluency, and adding great charm to delivery. The following passage should be studied from the rhythmical point of view. The atmosphere depends upon the speaker's awareness of the subtle changes of rhythm, and not less upon the sensitiveness with which he controls his accent-stress in delivery.

> The wilderness and the solitary place shall be glad for them; and the desert shall rejoice, and blossom as the rose.
> It shall blossom abundantly, and rejoice even with joy and singing: the glory of Lebanon shall be given unto it, the excellency of Carmel and Sharon, they shall see the glory of the Lord, and the excellency of our God.
> Strengthen ye the weak hands, and confirm the feeble knees.
> Say to them that are of a fearful heart, Be strong, fear not: behold, your God will come with vengeance, even God with a recompence; he will come and save you.

Then the eyes of the blind shall be opened, and the ears of the deaf shall be unstopped.

Then shall the lame man leap as an hart, and the tongue of the dumb sing: for in the wilderness shall waters break out, and streams in the desert.

And the parched ground shall become a pool, and the thirsty land springs of water: in the habitation of dragons, where each lay, shall be grass with reeds and rushes.

And an highway shall be there, and a way, and it shall be called The way of holiness; the unclean shall not pass over it; but it shall be for those: the wayfaring men, though fools, shall not err therein.

No lion shall be there, nor any ravenous beast shall go up thereon, it shall not be found there; but the redeemed shall walk there:

And the ransomed of the Lord shall return, and come to Zion with songs and everlasting joy upon their heads: they shall obtain joy and gladness, and sorrow and sighing shall flee away.

Isaiah xxxv.

As rhythmical speech is possible only through syllabic stress, it is natural that unaccented syllables must be subordinated, and this subordination affects the vowel quality. The vowel of an accented syllable has a real phonetic value. The vowel of an unaccented syllable is neutralised. Thus the neutral vowel is the commonest vowel in English speech. In the very obvious example,

The golden plover sings her song,

Her song about the Spring.

it will be noticed that all the unaccented syllables contain neutral vowels,

ðə gouldən plʌvə siŋz hə sɔŋ

hə sɔŋ əbaut ðə spriŋ.

This matter needs careful attention, especially when studying speech formation. Clear speech does not depend

upon a phonetic value being given to all syllables indiscriminately. It is principally the result of crisp
consonants throughout, and accurately formed vowels
in the stressed syllables only.

In the establishment of meaning, STRESS is all important.
The meaning of the phrase can be sensitively conveyed
only when differing degrees of stress indicate the relative
value of various words. It is possible to grade the stress
in a simple sentence, for example, "The INKPOT was
nearly FULL when I *finished using* it." As a rule this
relative valuation is adjusted without conscious control,
provided the meaning is fully understood; but when the
matter is of great importance, the meaning obscure, or
the structure involved, it becomes necessary to use a more
conscious stress control. Practice on passages, such as
the following, is recommended.

> The liberty of a people consists in being governed by laws
> which they have made themselves, under whatsoever form
> it be of government; the liberty of a private man, in being
> master of his own time and actions, as far as may consist
> with the laws of God, and of his country. Of this latter,
> only, we are here to discourse, and to inquire what estate
> of life does best seat us in the possession of it. This liberty
> of our actions is such a fundamental privilege of human
> nature, that God himself, notwithstanding all his infinite
> power and right over us, permits us to enjoy it, and that too
> after a forfeiture made by the rebellion of Adam. He takes
> so much care for the entire preservation of it to us, that he
> suffers neither his providence nor eternal decree to break
> or infringe it. Nor for our time, the same God, to whom
> we are but tenants-at-will for the whole, requires but the
> seventh part of it to be paid to him as a small quit-rent in
> acknowledgment of his title. It is man only that has the
> impudence to demand our whole time, though he neither
> gave it, nor can restore it, nor is able to pay any considerable
> value for the least part of it. This birth-right of mankind
> above all other creatures, some are forced by hunger to sell,

like Esau, for bread and broth; but the greatest part of men make such a bargain for the delivery up of themselves, as Thamur did for Judah; instead of a kid, the necessary provisions for human life, they are contented to do it for rings and bracelets. The great dealers in this world may be divided into the ambitious, the covetous, and the voluptuous; and that all these men sell themselves to be slaves, though to the vulgar it may seem a Stoical paradox, will appear to the wise so plain and obvious, that they scarce think it deserves the labour of argumentation.

Of Liberty, COWLEY.

EMPHASIS might be regarded as an extra measure of stress, occasioned by strong appeal, emotional intensity, or the climactic point of an argument, when it is necessary to focus attention upon a carefully chosen word, intended to be used with great effect. It is governed by understanding and requires feeling. In its artistic application, the speaker needs clear perception as well as emotional awareness. The following is a suitable exercise.

> The war, that for a space did fail,
> Now trebly thundering swell'd the gale,
> And *Stanley*! was the cry;—
> A light on Marmion's visage spread,
> And fired his glazing eye:
> With dying hand above his head,
> He shook the fragment of his blade,
> And shouted "*Victory*!—
> *Charge,* Chester, *Charge*! *On*, Stanley, *on*!"
> Were the last words of Marmion.

From *Marmion*, SCOTT.

Strong emphasis, in almost every case, is associated with the emotional pause, which by isolating the important word, increases the sense of emphasis, as will now be obvious if the examples on page 44 are reviewed.

D

The methods discussed so far are not the only means of sense expression. There is now, for instance, the much less tangible use of TUNE to be examined—the melodic rise and fall of vocal pitch while speaking. When considered in connection with a phrase, this tune is known as INTONATION. In connection with a word or syllable, it is known as INFLECTION. It is not possible to lay down hard and fast rules about this matter as it varies greatly among individual speakers. Several "laws" can be stated, but the speaker must rely upon spontaneous feeling and upon his own personal interpretation. Unlike phrasing and stress, there is no clear method of accurately giving a written indication of intonation. Speech does not move, as song, from one note to another on a clearly defined diatonic scale; the voice "glides", now up, now down, to and from pitches appropriate to feeling. The melodic content of human speech defies accurate representation. Even though this subject can now be studied scientifically with the aid of electronic apparatus, such investigation seems only to emphasise the wide difference of individual application.

Careful investigation has, however, resulted in the stating of several fundamentals which are worth remembering. Those dealing with inflection will be given first.

Inflection may be either SIMPLE, that is with an upward *or* downward glide only; or it may be COMPOUND, with one or more upward *and* downward glides on a single word.

Simple inflections are associated with straightforward utterance, the rising inflection indicating lack of conclusion; the falling inflection indicating finality, either relative or absolute. For example, a real question always finishes with a rising inflection, while the reply is spoken on a falling inflection indicating conclusiveness, as in

"Are you going now?" . . . "Yes."

A compound inflection is employed to supplement the face value of a word. When more than the dictionary definition of a word is implied, the subtlety may best be suggested by using a compound inflection. In the example just given, the reply could be made to sound much less certain if spoken on a compound inflection,

"Are you going now?" . . . "Yes." (In which case it would not be necessary to add, "but I can't be sure", as this is clearly suggested by the inflection.)

Much useful experience can be gained by practice on one word, giving a number of different interpretations by various inflections. For instance, take the one word "father", and speak it as if to suggest—

(a) Recognition when father's arrival had been expected.

(b) Recognition when his arrival had not been expected.

(c) Recognition when his arrival had been considered impossible.

(d) Recognition when he arrives at a most embarrassing moment.

(e) Recognition when he arrives to be congratulated on some great achievement.

(f) Recognition when his arrival means your deliverance.

(g) As an exclamation after he has "let down" his family badly.

(h) As an exclamation during conversation after his death when his goodness to the family is being recalled,

and any other situations you can invent. It will soon become apparent that with flexibility of inflection you can express, in a word or two of speech, more than could be stated in sentences of writing.

Irony, sarcasm, scorn and similar figures rely on the use of compound inflections, and in antithesis the compound inflection is used in association with the negative clause, while the positive is strengthened by a simple inflection—"I didn't say shoes; I said boots". There are many opportunities of exploiting the use of compound inflections in the following passage.

Shylock.

> Signior Antonio, many a time and oft,
> In the Rialto, you have rated me
> About my monies and my usances:
> Still have I borne it with a patient shrug,
> For sufferance is the badge of all our tribe:
> You call me misbeliever, cut-throat dog,
> And spit upon my Jewish gaberdine,
> And all for use of that which is mine own.
> Well then, it now appears, you need my help:
> Go to then; you come to me, and you say,
> "Shylock, we would have monies": you say so;
> You, that did void your rheum upon my beard,
> And foot me, as you spurn a stranger cur
> Over your threshold: monies is your suit.
> What should I say to you? Should I not say,
> "Hath a dog money? is it possible
> A cur can lend three thousand ducats?" or
> Shall I bend low, and in a bondman's key,
> With bated breath and whispering humbleness,
> Say this,—
> "Fair sir, you spit on me on Wednesday last;
> You spurn'd me such a day; another time
> You call'd me dog; and for these courtesies
> I'll lend you thus much monies"?

From The Merchant of Venice, SHAKESPEARE.

In addition to suggesting incompleteness or completeness by the direction, an inflection shows degree of intensity by the length of its glide. A mild affirmative in reply to a question of small importance would perhaps pass through only a semitone, *e.g.* "This is your pencil, isn't it?" . . . "Yes." If the same word "Yes" is used at the end of a long argument, when real finality and certainty are to be registered, it would not be unusual for the voice to pass through an octave, *e.g.*, ". . . and that is your last word?" . . . "Yes!"

These laws might be summarised as the laws of suspense and conclusion. For doubt, uncertainty and incon- clusiveness, the inflection is a rising one. For certainty, finality and conclusion, the falling inflection is employed. The interval through which the voice passes increases with the intensity.

Naturally there is a close relationship between inflection and pause. The cessation of voice during a pause could (and unless mental concentration is intense, at times unfortunately does) weaken continuity. The psycho- logical effect of the rising inflection is to suspend thought until it is desired to conclude. By reverting to the examples previously given, the relationship between pause and inflection will be clearly seen. The following exercise will also be of use.

Though fond of many acquaintances, I desire an intimacy only with a few. The man in black, whom I have often mentioned, is one whose friendship I could wish to acquire, because he possesses my esteem. His manners, it is true, are tinctured with some strange inconsistencies, and he may justly be termed a humourist in a nation of humourists. Though he is generous even to profusion, he affects to be thought a prodigy of parsimony and prudence; though his conversation be replete with the most sordid and selfish maxims, his heart is dilated with the most unbounded love. I have known him profess himself a man-hater, while his cheek was glowing with compassion; and, while his looks were softened into pity, I have heard him use the language of the most unbounded ill-nature. Some affect humanity and tenderness, others boast of having such dispositions from nature; but he is the only man I ever knew who seemed ashamed of his natural benevolence. He takes as much pains to hide his feelings, as any hypocrite would to conceal his indifference; but on every unguarded moment the mask drops off, and reveals him to the most superficial observer.

In one of our late excursions into the country, happening to discourse upon the provision that was made for the poor in England, he seemed amazed how any of his countrymen could be so foolishly weak as to relieve occasional objects of charity, when the laws had made such ample provision for their support. "In every parish-house," says he, "the poor are supplied with food, clothes, fire, and a bed to lie on; they want no more, I desire no more myself; yet still they seem discontented. I am surprised at the inactivity of our magistrates, in not taking up such vagrants, who are only a weight upon the industrious; I am surprised that the people are found to relieve them, when they must be at the same time sensible that it, in some measure, encourages idleness, extravagance, and imposture. Were I to advise any man for whom I had the least regard, I would caution him by all means not to be imposed upon by their false pretences: let me assure you, Sir, they are imposters, every one of them, and rather merit a prison than relief."

He was proceeding in this strain, earnestly to dissuade me from an imprudence of which I am seldom guilty, when an old man, who still had about him the remnants of tattered finery, implored our compassion. He assured us that he was no common beggar, but forced into the shameful profession, to support a dying wife and five hungry children. Being prepossessed against such falsehoods, his story had not the least influence upon me; but it was quite otherwise with the man in black; I could see it visibly operate upon his countenance, and effectually interrupt his harangue. I could easily perceive, that his heart burned to relieve the five starving children, but he seemed ashamed to discover his weakness to me. While he thus hesitated between compassion and pride, I pretended to look another way, and he seized this opportunity of giving the poor petitioner a piece of silver, bidding him at the same time, in order that I should hear, go work for his bread, and not tease passengers with such impertinent falsehoods for the future.

As he had fancied himself quite unperceived, he continued, as we proceeded, to rail against beggars with as much animosity as before; he threw in some episodes on his own amazing prudence and economy, with his profound skill in discovering imposters; he explained the manner in which he would deal with beggars were he a magistrate, hinted at enlarging some of the prisons for their reception, and told two stories of ladies that were robbed by beggarmen. He was beginning a third to the same purpose, when a sailor with a wooden leg once more crossed our walks, desiring our pity, and blessing our limbs. I was for going on without taking any notice, but my friend looking wistfully upon the poor petitioner, bid me stop, and he would show me with how much ease he could at any time detect an imposter.

He now, therefore, assumed a look of importance, and in an angry tone began to examine the sailor, demanding in what engagement he was thus disabled and rendered unfit for service. The sailor replied, in a tone as angrily as he, that he had been an officer on board a private ship of war, and that he had lost his leg abroad, in defence of those who did nothing at home. At this reply, all my friend's importance vanished in a moment; he had not a single question more to ask; he only studied what method he could take to relieve him unobserved. He had, however, no easy part to act, as he was obliged to preserve the appearance of ill-nature before me, and yet relieve himself by relieving the sailor. Casting, therefore, a furious look upon some bundles of chips which the fellow carried in a string at his back, my friend demanded how he sold his matches; but not waiting for a reply, desired, in a surly tone, to have a shilling's worth. The sailor seemed at first surprised at his demand, but soon recollected himself, and presenting his whole bundle, "Here, master," says he, "take all my cargo, and a blessing into the bargain."

It is impossible to describe with what an air of triumph my friend marched off with his new purchase: he assured me, that he was firmly of opinion that those fellows must have stolen their goods, who could thus afford to sell them at half value. He informed me of several different uses to which those chips might be applied; he expatiated largely upon the savings that would result from lighting candles with a match, instead of thrusting them into the fire. He averred, that he would as soon have parted with a tooth as his money to those vagabonds, unless for some valuable consideration. I cannot tell how long this panegyric upon frugality and matches might have continued, had not his attention been called off by another object more distressful than either of the former. A woman in rags, with one child in her arms, and another on her back, was attempting to sing ballads, with but such a mournful voice, that it was difficult to determine whether she was singing or crying. A wretch, who in the deepest distress still aimed at good-humour, was an object my friend was by no means capable of withstanding: his vivacity and his discourse were instantly interrupted; upon this occasion, his very dissimulation had forsaken him. Even in my presence he immediately applied his hands to his pockets, in order to relieve her; but guess his confusion when he found he had already given away all the money he carried about him to former objects. The misery painted in the woman's visage was not half so strongly expressed as the agony in his. He continued to search for some time, but to no purpose, till, at length recollecting himself, with a face of ineffable good-nature, as he had no money, he put into her hands his shilling's worth of matches.

The Man in Black, GOLDSMITH.

Intonation, already spoken of as the melody of speech, might also be regarded as the combination of the various inflections on which the separate words are spoken. Generally, this "speech-melody" tends to rise to the important word and to fall as the word is spoken; but it does not fall to the same level of finality reserved for the end of the sentence, unless the word is, in fact, the final word. Intonation and inflection should, therefore, be studied in conjunction with stress and emphasis; in fact it should now be clear that no single factor in vocal expression can be examined without reference to most of the others. The meanings of words are always extended by sensitive inflection and subtle intonation. The following example might be spoken in at least six different ways by varying the stress and inflection, and therefore the intonation. This exercise also shows how a negative phrase usually carries a rising intonation, except in a strongly emphatic form. It also serves to illustrate the way in which emphasis by stress need not be so strong when a compound inflection is employed.

Exercise. That is not my sister's bag.

Interpretation.	Implied meaning.
That is not my sister's bag.	(*This* one is.)
That *is* not my sister's bag.	(But it *was* until she gave it away.)
That is NOT my sister's bag.	(I've told you before that it isn't!)
That is not *my* sister's bag.	(It is *your* sister's.)
That is not my *sister's* bag.	(It belongs to my aunt.)
That is not my sister's bag.	(But the contents of it are her's.)

This very simple example is sufficient to show how complicated this matter is and how futile it would be to attempt to lay down dogmatic laws. It is a matter of understanding and feeling, rather than technique. With a clear conception of the sense content, and a desire to impart the knowledge with conviction, the subtleties will be expressed sensitively.

PITCH is not so difficult to understand as it is bound up, quite clearly, with the general mood of the passage under consideration. Ordinary conversation is, as a rule, spoken on a pitch about the middle of the speaker's vocal range. If excitement or any other exhilarating influence is felt, then generally the pitch tends to rise, while sadness or any other depressing emotion would usually be expressed on a lower pitch.

The effect of the subject-matter on pitch is usually an unconscious one, but the speaker should consciously consider two limiting factors. Firstly, he must not allow his emotions to carry his voice above, nor allow his voice to fall below, the limits of easily produced tone. Secondly, he may have to affect a compromise by modifying his pitch to suit the acoustic conditions under which he is speaking. This last consideration is a matter of constant trial and error during the early days of practice, after which the experience of the speaker will enable him to find the best "carrying" pitch during the first several sentences spoken. Two excerpts are suggested as examples which seem to require low and medium pitches respectively. The higher pitches of a speaker's voice are rarely sustained for a period of sufficient duration to warrant an exercise for this purpose exclusively.

It was midnight, but the night was bright enough for the unhappy purpose they came about. All six entered the fatal square, the chairman keeping the gate, lest any person should disturb the duel. After not more than a couple of minutes, a cry caused Esmond to look round. He ran up to the place, where he saw his dear master was down.

My Lord Mohun was standing over him. "Are you much hurt, Frank?" he asked in a hollow voice.

"I believe I'm a dead man," my lord said from the ground.

"No! no! not so," says the other. "I call Heaven to witness, Frank Esmond, that I would have asked your pardon had you but given me a chance. I swear no one was to blame but me, and that my lady——"

"Hush!" says my poor lord viscount, lifting himself up, "don't let her name be heard in the quarrel. It was a dispute about the cards!—Harry, my boy, I loved thee, and thou must watch over my little Frank, and carry this little heart to my wife."

They brought him to a surgeon in Long Acre, the house was wakened up, and the victim carried in.

Lord Castlewood was laid on a bed, very pale and ghastly, with that fixed fatal look in his eyes which betokens death. Faintly beckoning all away from him, he cried, "Only Harry Esmond," and his hand fell powerless on the coverlet.

"Thou art but a priest, Harry!" he gasped, with a faint smile and pressure of his cold hand. "Let me make thee a death-bed confession."

With sacred Death waiting, as it were, at the bedfoot, as an awful witness of his words, the poor dying soul gasped out his last wishes, his contrition for his faults, and his charity towards the world he was leaving. The ecclesiastic we had sent for arrived, hearing which, my lord asked, squeezing Esmond's hand, to be left alone with him.

At the end of an hour the priest came out of the room looking hard at Esmond, and holding a paper.

"He is on the brink of God's awful judgment," the priest whispered. "He has made his breast clean to me."

"God knows," sobbed out Esmond, seemingly unconscious of the words, "my dearest lord has only done me kindness all his life."

The priest put the paper into Esmond's hand.

He looked at it. It swam before his eyes. "'Tis a confession," he said.

"'Tis as you please," said the priest.

There was a fire in the room. Esmond went to the fire and threw the paper into it.

"'Tis only a confession, Mr Atterbury. Let us go to him."

They went into the next chamber; the dawn had broke, and showed the poor lord's pale face and wild appealing eyes, which wore the awful look of coming dissolution. He turned his sick eyes towards Esmond.

"My lord viscount," says the priest, "Mr Esmond hath burned the paper."

"My dearest master," Esmond cried.

My lord viscount sprung up in his bed and flung his arms round Esmond. "God—bl—bless" was all he said. The blood rushed from his mouth. He was no more.

"Benedicti Benedicentes," whispers the priest.

And Esmond groaned "Amen."

From *Henry Esmond*, THACKERAY.

Mankind, says a Chinese manuscript, which my friend M. was obliging enough to read and explain to me, for the first seventy thousand ages ate their meat raw, clawing or biting it from the living animal, just as they do in Abyssinia to this day. This period is not obscurely hinted at by their great Confucius in the second chapter of his Mundane Mutations, where he designates a kind of golden age by the term Cho-fang, literally the Cooks' Holiday. The manuscript goes on to say, that the art of roasting, or rather broiling (which I take to be the elder brother), was accidentally discovered in the manner following. The swine-herd, Ho-ti, having gone out into the woods one morning, as his manner was, to collect mast for his hogs, left his cottage in the care of his eldest son Bo-bo, a great lubberly boy, who being fond of playing with fire, as younkers of his age commonly are, let some sparks escape into a bundle of straw, which kindling quickly spread the conflagration over every part of their poor mansion, till it was reduced to ashes. Together with the cottage (a sorry antediluvian makeshift of a building, you may think it), what was of much more importance, a fine litter of new-farrowed pigs, no less than nine in number, perished. China pigs have been esteemed a luxury all over the East, from the remotest periods that we read of. Bo-bo was in the utmost consternation, as you may think, not so much for the sake of the tenement, which his father and he could easily build up again with a few dry branches, and the labour of an hour or two, at any time, as for the loss of the pigs. While he was thinking what he should say to his father, and wringing his hands over the smoking remnants of one of those untimely sufferers, an odour assailed his nostrils, unlike any scent which he had before experienced. What could it proceed from?—not from the burnt cottage—he had smelt that smell before— indeed, this was by no means the first accident of this kind which had occurred through the negligence of this unlucky young firebrand. Much less did it resemble that of any known herb, weed, or flower. A premonitory moistening at the same time overflowed his nether lip. He knew not what to think. He next stooped down to feel the pig, if there were any signs of life in it. He burnt his fingers, and to cool them he applied them in his booby fashion to his mouth. Some of the crumbs of the scorched skin had come away with his fingers, and for the first time in his life (in the world's life indeed, for before him no man had known it) he tasted—crackling! Again he felt and fumbled at the pig. It did not burn him so much now, still he licked his fingers from a sort of habit. The truth at length broke into his slow understanding, that it was the pig that smelt so, and the pig that tasted so delicious; and surrendering himself up to the new-born pleasure, he fell to tearing up whole handfuls of the scorched skin with the flesh next it, and was cramming it down his throat in his beastly fashion, when his sire entered amid the smoking rafters, armed with retributory cudgel, and finding how affairs stood, began to rain blows upon the young rogue's shoulders, as thick as hailstones, which Bo-bo heeded not any more than if they had been flies. The tickling pleasure, which he experienced in his lower regions, had rendered him quite callous to any inconveniences he might feel in those remote quarters. His father might lay on, but he could not beat him from his pig, till he had fairly made an end of it, when, becoming a little more sensible of his situation, something like the following dialogue ensued.

"You graceless whelp, what have you got there devouring?

Is it not enough that you have burnt me down three houses
with your dog's tricks, and be hanged to you! but you must
be eating fire, and I know not what—what have you got
there, I say?"

"O father, the pig, the pig! do come and taste how nice
the burnt pig eats."

The ears of Ho-ti tingled with horror. He cursed his son,
and he cursed himself that ever he should beget a son that
should eat burnt pig.

Bo-bo, whose scent was wonderfully sharpened since
morning, soon raked out another pig, and fairly rending it
asunder, thrust the lesser half by main force into the fists
of Ho-ti, still shouting out, "Eat, eat, eat the burnt pig,
father, only taste—O Lord!"—with such-like barbarous
ejaculations, cramming all the while as if he would choke.

Ho-ti trembled in every joint while he grasped the
abominable thing, wavering whether he should not put his
son to death for an unnatural young monster, when the
crackling scorching his fingers, as it had done his son's,
and applying the same remedy to them, he in his turn
tasted some of its flavour, which, make what sour mouths he
would for a pretence, proved not altogether displeasing to
him. In conclusion (for the manuscript here is a little
tedious), both father and son fairly set down to the mess,
and never left off till they had despatched all that remained
of the litter.

Bo-bo was strictly enjoined not to let the secret escape,
for the neighbours would certainly have stoned them for a
couple of abominable wretches, who could think of improving upon the good meat which God had sent them. Nevertheless, strange stories got about. It was observed that
Ho-ti's cottage was burnt down now more frequently than
ever. Nothing but fires from this time forward. Some
would break out in broad day, others in the night-time.
As often as the sow farrowed, so sure was the house of Ho-ti
to be in a blaze; and Ho-ti himself, which was the more
remarkable, instead of chastening his son, seemed to grow
more indulgent to him than ever. At length they were
watched, the terrible mystery discovered, and father and

son summoned to take their trial at Pekin, then an inconsiderable assize town. Evidence was given, the obnoxious food itself produced in court, and verdict about to be pronounced, when the foreman of the jury begged that some of the burnt pig, of which the culprits stood accused, might be handed into the box. He handled it, and they all handled it; and burning their fingers, as Bo-bo and his father had done before them, and nature prompting to each of them the same remedy, against the face of all the facts, and the clearest charge which judge had ever given— to the surprise of the whole court, townsfolk, strangers, reporters, and all present—without leaving the box, or any manner of consultation whatever, they brought in a simultaneous verdict of Not Guilty.

The judge, who was a shrewd fellow, winked at the manifest iniquity of the decision: and when the court was dismissed, went privily and bought up all the pigs that could be had for love or money. In a few days his lordship's town-house was observed to be on fire. The thing took wing, and now there was nothing to be seen but fires in every direction. Fuel and pigs grew enormously dear all over the district. The insurance offices, one and all, shut up shop. People built slighter and slighter every day, until it was feared that the very science of architecture would in no long time be lost to the world. Thus this custom of firing houses continued, till in process of time, says my manuscript, a sage arose, like our Locke, who made a discovery that the flesh of swine, or indeed of any other animal, might be cooked (burnt, as they called it) without the necessity of consuming a whole house to dress it. Then first began the rude form of a gridiron. Roasting by the string or spit came in a century or two later, I forget in whose dynasty. By slow degrees, concludes the manuscript, do the most useful, and seemingly the most obvious, arts make their way among mankind.

Without placing too implicit faith in the account above given, it must be agreed that if a worthy pretext for so dangerous an experiment as setting houses on fire (especially in those days) could be assigned in favour of any culinary

object, that pretext and excuse might be found in ROAST
PIG.

From A Dissertation upon Roast Pig, LAMB.

Pace also is governed consciously by consideration of
two factors. The acoustics of an over-resonant room
necessitate a rather slower pace than normal, and there
is usually a limit to the speed at which the speech organs
of an individual will respond accurately and without
apparent effort. This articulatory limitation may be
reduced by practice, but there is always a limit, setting
a pace which must not be exceeded. In a less conscious
way the pace is dictated by the feeling for the matter being
spoken. Slower pace indicates thoughtful consideration,
despondency and similar emotions. Rhythm has a great
deal to do with pace, but for the present the following
exercises should be read at the pace which seems to be
most consistent with the sense and mood.

> And slowly answer'd Arthur from the barge;
> "The old order changeth, yielding place to new,
> And God fulfils himself in many ways,
> Lest one good custom should corrupt the world.
> Comfort thyself: what comfort is in me?
> I have lived my life, and that which I have done
> May He within himself make pure! but thou,
> If thou shouldst never see my face again,
> Pray for my soul. More things are wrought by prayer
> Than this world dreams of. Wherefore let thy voice
> Rise like a mountain for me night and day.
> For what are men better than sheep or goats
> That nourish a blind life within the brain,
> If, knowing God, they lift not hands of prayer
> Both for themselves and those who call them friend?
> For so the whole round earth is every way
> Bound by gold chains about the feet of God.
> But now farewell. I am going a long way

With these thou seest—if indeed I go
(For all my mind is clouded with a doubt)—
To the island-valley of Avilion;
Where falls not hail, or rain, or any snow,
Nor ever wind blows loudly; but it lies
Deep-meadow'd, happy, fair with orchard lawns
And bowery hollows crown'd with summer sea,
Where I will heal me of my grievous wound."

So said he, and the barge with oar and sail
Moved from the brink, like some full-breasted swan
That, fluting a wild carol ere her death,
Ruffles her pure cold plume, and takes the flood
With swarthy webs.   Long stood Sir Bedivere
Revolving many memories, till the hull
Look'd one black dot against the verge of dawn,
And on the mere the wailing died away.

But when the moan had past for evermore,
The stillness of the dead world's winter dawn
Amazed him, and he groan'd, "The King is gone."
And therewithal came on him the weird rhyme,
"From the great deep to the great deep he goes."

Whereat he slowly turn'd and slowly clomb
The last hard footsteps of that iron crag;
Thence mark'd the black hull moving yet, and cried,
"He passes to be King among the dead,
And after healing of his grievous wound
He comes again; but—if he come no more—
O me, be yon dark Queens in yon black boat,
Who shriek'd and wail'd, the three whereat we gazed
On that high day, when, clothed with living light,
They stood before his throne in silence, friends
Of Arthur, who should help him at his need?"

Then from the dawn it seem'd there came, but faint
As from beyond the limit of the world,
Like the last echo born of a great cry,
Sounds, as if some fair city were one voice
Around a king returning from his wars.

E

Thereat once more he moved about and clomb
Ev'n to the highest he could climb, and saw,
Straining his eyes beneath an arch of hand,
Or thought he saw, the speck that bare the King,
Down that long water opening on the deep
Somewhere far off, pass on and on, and go
From less to less and vanish into light.
And the new sun rose bringing the new year.

From *The Passing of Arthur*, TENNYSON.

An alehouse-keeper, near Islington, who had long lived at the sign of the French King, upon the commencement of the last war pulled down his old sign, and put up that of the Queen of Hungary. Under the influence of her red face and golden sceptre he continued to sell ale, till she was no longer the favourite of his customers; he changed her, therefore, some time ago, for the King of Prussia, who may probably be changed, in turn, for the next great man that shall be set up for vulgar admiration.

In this manner the great are dealt out, one after the other, to the gazing crowd. When we have sufficiently wondered at one of them, he is taken in, and another exhibited in his room, who seldom holds his station long; for the mob are ever pleased with variety.

I must own, I have such an indifferent opinion of the vulgar, that I am ever led to suspect that merit which raises their shout; at least I am certain to find those great, and sometimes good men, who feel satisfaction in such acclamations, made worse by it; and history has too frequently taught me, that the head which has grown this day giddy with the roar of the million, has, the very next, been fixed upon a pole.

There is scarce a village in Europe, and not one university, that is not furnished with its little great men. The head of a petty corporation, who opposes the designs of a prince, who would tyrannically force his subjects to save their best clothes for Sundays; the puny pedant, who finds one undiscovered quality in the polypus, or describes an unheeded process in the skeleton of a mole, and whose mind, like his microscope, perceives nature only in detail; the rhymer, who makes smooth verses, and paints to our imagination when he should only speak to our hearts;— all equally fancy themselves walking forward to immortality, and desire the crowd behind them to look on. The crowd takes them at their word. Patriot, philosopher, and poet, are shouted in their train. "Where was there ever so much merit seen? no times so important as our own! Ages, yet unborn, shall gaze with wonder and applause!" To such music the important pigmy moves forward, bustling and swelling, and aptly compared to a puddle in a storm.

I have lived to see generals, who once had crowds hallooing after them wherever they went, who were bepraised by newspapers and magazines—those echoes of the voice of the vulgar—and yet they have long sunk into merited obscurity, with scarce even an epitaph left to flatter. A few years ago the herring-fishery employed all Grub-Street; it was the topic in every coffee-house, and the burden of every ballad. We were to drag up oceans of gold from the bottom of the sea; we were to supply all Europe with herrings upon our own terms. At present we hear no more of all this. We have fished up very little gold, that I can learn; nor do we furnish the world with herrings, as was expected. Let us wait but a few years longer, and we shall find all our expectations—a herring-fishery!

On Human Grandeur, GOLDSMITH.

Get up, get up for shame! The blooming morn
Upon her wings presents the god unshorn.
    See how Aurora throws her fair
    Fresh-quilted colours through the air:
    Get up, sweet slug-a-bed, and see
    The dew bespangling herb and tree!
Each flower has wept and bow'd toward the east
Above an hour since, yet you not drest;
    Nay! not so much as out of bed?
    When all the birds have matins said
    And sung their thankful hymns, 'tis sin,
    Nay, profanation, to keep in,

Whereas a thousand virgins on this day
Spring sooner than the lark, to fetch in May.

.   .   .   .

Come, let us go, while we are in our prime,
And take the harmless folly of the time!
    We shall grow old apace, and die
    Before we know our liberty.
    Our life is short, and our days run
    As fast away as does the sun.
And, as a vapour or a drop of rain,
Once lost, can ne'er be found again,
    So when or you or I are made
    A fable, song, or fleeting shade,
    All love, all liking, all delight
    Lies drown'd with us in endless night.
Then, while time serves, and we are but decaying,
Come, my Corinna, come, let's go a-Maying.

From *Corinna's Going a-Maying*, HERRICK.

Parenthesis offers excellent opportunities of applying the technique of phrasing, pause, pitch and pace simultaneously. The parenthetical phrase is best subordinated by (*a*) separating it by pauses from the rest of the sentence, speaking it (*b*) at a slightly faster pace, and (*c*) on a somewhat lower pitch. After the parenthesis the speech is resumed on the dominant pitch and pace in keeping with the complete sentence.

In the example which follows, the intonation, pitch and pace should be continuous in "For her hair was now as white as snow". The parenthesis, "which previously had been a lustrous brown", must be given its own appropriate expression. The combination of the two then take the form which well might be represented—

FOR HER HAIR,   WAS NOW AS WHITE AS SNOW.
        which previously had
        been a lustrous brown,

The excerpt from the essay by Charles Lamb, on page 60, holds many opportunities to apply the technique just suggested.

Another means of expression is TONE COLOUR. Every individual voice has its own particular tone quality, based principally upon the characteristics of the resonators, and also upon the effectiveness with which these are utilised in the production of tone, which will be discussed later.

More important for our present purpose, however, is the fact that the characteristic tone of any one individual can be varied between wide limits according to the fluctuating intensity and varying mood of his emotions. Change of tone colour is, therefore, the result of an imaginative approach, and the changing emotions will be found to stimulate an immediate reaction vocally by warm, tender, hard, cold, brittle and other appropriate tonal variations. The following exercises are intended to demonstrate the wide range of themes necessitating many degrees of tone colour for their expression.

> Paul had never risen from his little bed. He lay there, listening to the noises in the street, quite tranquilly; not caring much how the time went, but watching it, and watching everything about him with observing eyes.
>
> When the sunbeams struck into his room through the rustling blinds, and quivered on the opposite wall like golden water, he knew that evening was coming on, and that the sky was red and beautiful. As the reflection died away, and a gloom went creeping up the wall, he watched it deepen, deepen, deepen into night. Then he thought how the long streets were dotted with lamps, and how the peaceful stars were shining overhead. His fancy had a strange tendency to wander to the river, which he knew was flowing through the great city; and now he thought how black it was, and how deep it would look, reflecting the hosts of stars—and more than all, how steadily it rolled away to meet the sea.

As it grew later in the night, and footsteps in the street became so rare that he could hear them coming, count them as they passed, and lose them in the hollow distance, he would lie and watch the many-coloured ring about the candle, and wait patiently for day. His only trouble was the swift and rapid river. He felt forced, sometimes, to try to stop it—to stem it with his childish hands—to choke its way with sand—and when he saw it coming on, resistless, he cried out! But a word from Florence, who was always at his side, restored him to himself; and leaning his poor head upon her breast, he told Floy of his dream, and smiled.

When day began to dawn again, he watched for the sun; and when its cheerful light began to sparkle in the room, he pictured to himself—pictured! he saw—the high church towers rising up into the morning sky, the town reviving, waking, starting into life once more, the river glistening as it rolled (but rolling fast as ever), and the country bright with dew. Familiar sounds and cries came by degrees into the street below; the servants in the house were roused and busy; faces looked in at the door, and voices asked his attendants softly how he was. Paul always answered for himself, "I am better. I am a great deal better, thank you! Tell papa so!"

By little and little he got tired of the bustle of the day, the noise of carriages and carts, and people passing and re-passing; and would fall asleep, or be troubled with a restless and uneasy sense again—the child could hardly tell whether this were in his sleeping or his waking moments —of that rushing river. "Why, will it never stop, Floy?" he would sometimes ask her. "It is bearing me away, I think!"

But Floy could always soothe and reassure him; and it was his daily delight to make her lay her head down on his pillow, and take some rest.

"You are always watching me, Floy. Let me watch you now!" They would prop him up with cushions in a corner of his bed, and there he would recline the while she lay beside him; bending forward oftentimes to kiss her, and whispering to those who were near that she was tired, and how she had sat up so many nights beside him.

Thus, the flush of the day, in its heat and light, would gradually decline, and again the golden water would be dancing on the wall.

From *Dombey and Son*, DICKENS.

Brutus.

Romans, countrymen, and lovers! hear me for my cause, and be silent, that you may hear; believe me for mine honour and have respect to mine honour, that you may believe: censure me in your wisdom, and awake your senses, that you may the better judge. If there be any in this assembly, any dear friend of Cæsar's, to him I say, that Brutus' love to Cæsar was no less than his. If then that friend demand why Brutus rose against Cæsar, this is my answer: Not that I loved Cæsar less, but that I loved Rome more. Had you rather Cæsar were living and die all slaves, than that Cæsar were dead, to live all free men? As Cæsar loved me, I weep for him; as he was fortunate, I rejoice at it; as he was valiant, I honour him; but as he was ambitious, I slew him. There is tears for his love; joy for his fortune, honour for his valour; and death for his ambition. Who is here so base that would be a bondman? If any, speak; for him have I offended. Who is here so rude that would not be a Roman? If any, speak; for him have I offended. Who is here so vile that will not love his country? If any, speak; for him have I offended. I pause for a reply. None? Then none have I offended. I have done no more to Cæsar than you shall do to Brutus. The question of his death is enrolled in the Capitol; his glory not extenuated wherein he was worthy, nor his offences enforced, for which he suffered death. Here comes his body, mourned by Mark Antony: who, though he had no hand in his death, shall receive the benefit of his dying, a place in the commonwealth; as which of you shall not? With this I depart— that, as I slew my best lover for the good of Rome, I have the same dagger for myself, when it shall please my country to need my death. . . .

Good countrymen, let me depart alone,
And, for my sake, stay here with Antony;
Do grace to Cæsar's corpse, and grace his speech
Tending to Cæsar's glories; which Mark Antony,
By our permission, is allow'd to make.
I do entreat you, not a man depart,
Save I alone, till Antony have spoke.

From *Julius Cæsar*, SHAKESPEARE.

Marullus.

Wherefore rejoice?   What conquest brings he home?
What tributaries follow him to Rome,
To grace in captive bonds his chariot-wheels?
You blocks, you stones, you worse than senseless things!
O you hard hearts, you cruel men of Rome,
Knew you not Pompey?   Many a time and oft
Have you not climb'd up to walls and battlements,
To towers and windows, yea, to chimney-tops,
Your infants in your arms, and there have sat
The live-long day, with patient expectation,
To see great Pompey pass the streets of Rome:
And when you saw his chariot but appear,
Have you not made an universal shout,
That Tiber trembled underneath her banks,
To hear the replication of your sounds
Made in her concave shores?
And do you now put on your best attire?
And do you now cull out a holiday?
And do you now strew flowers in his way
That comes in triumph over Pompey's blood?
Begone!
Run to your houses, fall upon your knees,
Pray to the gods to intermit the plague
That needs must light on this ingratitude.

From *Julius Cæsar*, SHAKESPEARE.

Lorenzo.

> How sweet the moonlight sleeps upon this bank!
> Here will we sit, and let the sounds of music
> Creep in our ears: soft stillness and the night
> Become the touches of sweet harmony.
> Sit, Jessica; look how the floor of heaven
> Is thick inlaid with patines of bright gold;
> There's not the smallest orb which thou beholds't
> But in his motion like an angel sings,
> Still quiring to the young-eyed cherubins;
> Such harmony is in immortal souls,
> But whilst this muddy vesture of decay
> Doth grossly close it in, we cannot hear it.

> From *The Merchant of Venice*, SHAKESPEARE.

VOLUME of voice has not yet been mentioned. For the purposes of the present chapter it must be pointed out that degree of volume is dependent upon the necessity of audibility rather than upon expression of sense. It is better to develop sensitivity of expression before attempting to increase the power of voice. Quite naturally, however, there are gradations of volume to be made as meaning and mood change, but these should be carried out within the speaker's present capabilities. Later he will learn how to increase volume, and he will be able to modify this to suit the demands of any auditorium, without disturbing the relative arrangement of degrees from pianissimo to fortissimo. In connection with changing volume, the following is a good exercise.

King Henry.

> Once more unto the breach, dear friends, once more;
> Or close the wall up with our English dead!
> In peace there's nothing so becomes a man
> As modest stillness and humility:

But when the blast of war blows in our ears,
Then imitate the action of the tiger;
Stiffen the sinews, summon up the blood,
Disguise fair nature with hard-favour'd rage:
Then lend the eye a terrible aspect;
Let it pry through the portage of the head
Like the brass cannon; let the brow o'erwhelm it,
As fearfully as doth a galled rock
O'erhang and jutty his confounded base,
Swill'd with the wild and wasteful ocean.
Now set the teeth and stretch the nostril wide;
Hold hard the breath and bend up every spirit
To his full height!—On, on, you noblest English,
Whose blood is fet from fathers of war-proof!
Fathers that, like so many Alexanders,
Have in these parts from morn till even fought,
And sheathed their swords for lack of argument.
Dishonour not your mothers; now attest
That those whom you call'd fathers did beget you!
Be copy now to men of grosser blood,
And teach them how to war!—And you, good yeomen,
Whose limbs were made in England, shew us here
The mettle of your pasture; let us swear
That you are worth your breeding; which I doubt not;
For there is none of you so mean and base,
That hath not noble lustre in your eyes.
I see you stand like greyhounds in the slips,
Straining upon the start. The game's afoot:
Follow your spirit, and, upon this charge,
Cry "God for Harry! England! and Saint George!"

From *Henry V*, SHAKESPEARE.

MODULATION is the result of consistently co-ordinating
the modifications of all the foregoing technical devices in
order to convey meaning as sensitively as possible from
speaker to listener. Adequate modulation for any form
of public speaking is an acquired art, depending upon
constant practice until flexibility is attained, so that

imagination may assume control, giving life to the technical methods no longer consciously applied.

One of the principal applications of modulation is in connection with CLIMAX, without which no selection of any kind can be effectively presented. There are no hard and fast rules about the establishment of a strong climactic development. Some speakers adopt a rather obvious application of the technique already described, others rely more upon the increase of mental intensity. The balance finally decided upon, between vocal technique and psychological projection, must depend upon the speaker's own individual style and upon his personal interpretation.

Climax is reached, not by a steady ascent, but by a series of undulations. A clear example of this is to be noticed in the following example, in every verse of which there is a clearly discernable climax. The climax of the poem is the result of the combination of the progressive build-up of each stanza.

There was a sound of revelry by night,
And Belgium's capital had gathered then
Her Beauty and her Chivalry, and bright
The lamps shone o'er fair women and brave men;
A thousand hearts beat happily; and when
Music arose with its voluptuous swell,
Soft eyes look'd love to eyes which spake again,
And all went merry as a marriage bell;
But hush! hark! a deep sound strikes like a rising knell!

Did ye not hear it?—No; 'twas but the wind,
Or the car rattling o'er the stony street;
On with the dance! let joy be unconfined;
No sleep till morn, when Youth and Pleasure meet
To chase the glowing Hours with flying feet—
But hark!—that heavy sound breaks in once more,
As if the clouds its echo would repeat;

And nearer, clearer, deadlier than before!
Arm! Arm! it is—it is—the cannon's opening roar!

Within a window'd niche of that high hall
Sate Brunswick's fated chieftain; he did hear
That sound the first amidst the festival,
And caught its tone with Death's prophetic ear;
And when they smiled because he deem'd it near,
His heart more truly knew that peal too well
Which stretch'd his father on a bloody bier,
And roused the vengeance blood alone could quell,
He rush'd into the field, and, foremost fighting, fell.

Ah! then and there was hurrying to and fro,
And gathering tears, and trembling of distress,
And cheeks all pale, which but an hour ago
Blush'd at the praise of their own loveliness;
And there were sudden partings, such as press
The life from out young hearts, and choking sighs
Which ne'er might be repeated; who could guess
If ever more should meet those mutual eyes,
Since upon night so sweet such awful morn could rise!

And there was mounting in hot haste: the steed,
The mustering squadron, and the clattering car,
Went pouring forward with impetuous speed,
And swiftly forming in the ranks of war;
And the deep thunder peal on peal afar;
And near, the beat of the alarming drum
Roused up the soldier ere the morning star;
While throng'd the citizens with terror dumb,
Or whispering, with white lips—"The foe! they come!
 they come!"

And wild and high the "Cameron's gathering" rose!
The war-note of Lochiel, which Albyn's hills
Have heard, and heard, too, have her Saxon foes:—

How in the noon of night that pibroch thrills,
Savage and shrill! But with the breath which fills
Their mountain pipe, so fill the mountaineers
With the fierce native daring which instils
The stirring memory of a thousand years,
And Evan's, Donald's fame rings in each clansman's ears!

And Ardennes waves above them her green leaves,
Dewy with Nature's tear-drops as they pass,
Grieving, if aught inanimate e'er grieves,
Over the unreturning brave,—alas!
Ere evening to be trodden like the grass
Which now beneath them, but above shall grow
In its next verdure, when this fiery mass
Of living valour, rolling on the foe
And burning with light hope shall moulder cold and low.

Last noon beheld them full of lusty life,
Last eve in Beauty's circle proudly gay,
The midnight brought the signal-sound of strife,
The morn the marshalling in arms—the day
Battle's magnificently stern array!
The thunder-clouds close o'er it, which when rent
The earth is cover'd thick with other clay,
Which her own clay shall cover, heap'd and pent,
Rider and horse—friend, foe—in one red burial blent!

The Eve of Waterloo, LORD BYRON.

Before leaving the technical for the interpretational, some time should be spent on the following exercises, which should be studied carefully before any attempt is made to speak them. The various technical factors examined in this chapter should be exploited in order to reach a stage whereby the technique of expression will sensitively serve the mental conceptions and the emotional reactions of the speaker.

"Don't you think that," I asked the coachman, in the first stage out of London, "a very remarkable sky? I don't remember to have seen one like it."

"Nor I—not equal to it," he replied. "That's wind, sir. There'll be mischief done at sea, I expect, before long."

It was a mirky confusion—here and there blotted with a colour like the colour of the smoke from damp fuel—of flying clouds, tossed up on to most remarkable heaps, suggesting greater heights in the clouds than there were depths below them to the bottom of the deepest hollows in the earth, through which the wild moon seemed to plunge headlong, as if, in a dread disturbance of the laws of nature, she had lost her way and were frightened. There had been a wind all day; and it was rising then, with an extraordinary great sound. In another hour it had much increased, and the sky was more overcast, and it blew hard.

But as the night advanced, the clouds closing in and densely overspreading the whole sky, then very dark, it came on to blow harder and harder. It still increased, until our horses could scarcely face the wind. Many times, in the dark part of the night (it was then late in September, when the nights were not short), the leaders turned about, or came to a dead stop; and we were often in serious apprehension that the coach would be blown over. Sweeping gusts of rain came up before this storm, like showers of steel; and at those times, when there was any shelter of trees or lee walls to be got, we were fain to stop, in a sheer impossibility of continuing the struggle.

When the day broke, it blew harder and harder. I had been in Yarmouth when the seamen said it blew great guns; but I had never known the like of this, or anything approaching to it. We came to Ipswich—very late, having had to fight every inch of ground since we were ten miles out of London—and found a cluster of people in the market-place, who had risen from their beds in the night, fearful of falling chimneys. Some of these, congregating about the inn-yard while we changed horses, told us of great sheets of lead having been ripped off a high church tower, and flung into a by-street, which they then blocked up. Others had to tell of country people, coming in from neighbouring villages, who had seen great trees lying torn out of the earth, and whole ricks scattered about the roads and fields. Still, there was no abatement in the storm, but it blew harder.

As we struggled on, nearer and nearer to the sea, from which this mighty wind was blowing dead on shore, its force became more and more terrific. Long before we saw the sea, its spray was on our lips, and showered salt rain upon us. The water was out, over miles and miles of the flat country adjacent to Yarmouth; and every sheet and puddle lashed its banks, and had its stress of little breakers setting heavily towards us. When we came within sight of the sea, the waves on the horizon, caught at intervals above the rolling abyss, were like glimpses of another shore with towers and buildings. When at last we got into the town, the people came out to their doors, all aslant, and with streaming hair, making a wonder of the mail that had come through such a night.

I put up at the old inn, and went down to look at the sea; staggering along the street, which was strewn with sand and sea-weed, and with flying blotches of sea-foam, afraid of falling slates and tiles; and holding by people I met, at angry corners. Coming nearer the beach, I saw, not only the boatmen, but half the people of the town, lurking behind buildings; some now and then braving the fury of the storm to look away to sea, and blown sheer out of their courses in trying to get zigzag back.

Joining these groups, I found bewailing women whose husbands were away in herring or oyster boats, which there was too much reason to think might have foundered before they could run in anywhere for safety. Grizzled old sailors were among the people, shaking their heads, as they looked from water to sky, and muttering to one another; ship-owners, excited and uneasy; children, huddling together, and peering into older faces; even stout mariners, disturbed and anxious, levelling their glasses at the sea from behind places of shelter, as if they were surveying an enemy.

The tremendous sea itself, when I could find sufficient

pause to look at it, in the agitation of the blinding wind, the flying stones and sand, and the awful noise, confounded me. As the high watery walls came rolling in, and, at their highest, tumbled into surf, they looked as if the least would engulf the town. As the receding wave swept back with a hoarse roar, it seemed to scoop out deep caves in the beach, as if its purpose were to undermine the earth. When some white-headed billows thundered on, and dashed themselves to pieces before they reached the land, every fragment of the late whole seemed possessed by the full might of its wrath, rushing to be gathered to the composition of another monster. Undulating hills were changed to valleys, undulating valleys (with a solitary storm-bird sometimes skimming through them) were lifted up to the hills; masses of water shivered and shook the beach with a booming sound; every shape tumultuously rolled on, as soon as made, to change its shape and place, and beat another shape and place away; the ideal shore on the horizon, with its towers and buildings, rose and fell; the clouds flew fast and thick; I seemed to see a rending and upheaving of all nature.

From *David Copperfield*, DICKENS.

Studies serve for delight, for ornament, and for ability. Their chief use for delight is in privateness and retiring; for ornament, is in discourse; and for ability, is in the judgment and disposition of business; for expert men can execute, and perhaps judge of particulars, one by one; but the general counsels, and the plots and marshalling of affairs come best from those that are learned. To spend too much time in studies, is sloth; to use them too much for ornament, is affectation; to make judgment wholly by their rules, is the humour of a scholar: they perfect nature, and are perfected by experience: for natural abilities are like natural plants, that need pruning by study; and studies themselves do give forth directions too much at large, except they be bounded by experience. Crafty men condemn studies, simple men admire them, and wise men use them; for they teach not their own use; but that is a wisdom without them and above them, won by observation. Read not to contradict and confute, nor to believe and take for granted, nor to find talk and discourse, but to weigh and consider. Some books are to be tasted, others to be swallowed, and some few to be chewed and digested; that is, some books are to be read only in parts; others to be read but not curiously; and some few to be read wholly, and with diligence and attention. Some books also may be read by deputy, and extracts made of them by others; but that would be only in the less important arguments and the meaner sort of books; else distilled books are, like common distilled waters, flashy things. Reading maketh a full man; conference a ready man; and writing an exact man; and, therefore, if a man write little, he had need have a great memory; if he confer little, he had need have a present wit; and if he read little, he had need have much cunning, to seem to know that he doth not. Histories make men wise; poets, witty; the mathematics, subtle; natural philosophy, deep; moral, grave; logic and rhetoric, able to contend: "Abeunt studia in mores"; nay, there is no stand or impediment in the wit, but may be brought out by fit studies: like as diseases of the body may have appropriate exercises; bowling is good for the stone and reins, shooting for the lungs and breast, gentle walking for the stomach, riding for the head and the like; so if a man's wit be wandering, let him study the mathematics; for in demonstrations, if his wit be called away never so little, he must begin again; if his wit be not apt to distinguish or find difference, let him study the schoolmen; for they are "Cymini sectores". If he be not apt to beat over matters, and to call up one thing to prove and illustrate another, let him study the lawyers' cases: so every defect of the mind may have a special receipt.

Of Studies, FRANCIS BACON.

As one funny young gentleman will serve as a sample of all funny young gentlemen, we purpose merely to note down the conduct and behaviour of an individual specimen of this class.

We were all seated round a blazing fire which crackled pleasantly, when there came a postman's knock at the door, so violent and sudden, that it startled the whole circle, and actually caused two or three very interesting and most unaffected young ladies to scream aloud, until they had been several times assured by their respective adorers, that they were in no danger. We were about to remark that it was surely beyond post-time, when our host, who had hitherto been paralysed with wonder, sank into a chair in a perfect ecstasy of laughter, and offered to lay twenty pounds that it was that droll dog Griggins. He had no sooner said this, than the majority of the company burst into a roar of laughter, and gave vent to various exclamations of—To be sure it must be Griggins, and How like him that was, and What spirits he was always in!

Not having the happiness to know Griggins, we became extremely desirous to see so pleasant a fellow, when the door opened, and Mr Griggins being announced, presented himself, amidst another shout of laughter. This welcome he acknowledged by sundry contortions of countenance, which were so extremely successful that one stout gentleman rolled upon an ottoman in a paroxysm of delight, protesting, with many gasps, that if somebody didn't make that fellow Griggins leave off, he would be the death of him, he knew.

When he had quite exhausted all beholders, Mr Griggins received the welcomes and congratulations of the circle, and went through the needful introductions with much ease and many puns. This ceremony over, he avowed his intention of sitting in somebody's lap unless the young ladies made room for him on the sofa, which being done, after a great deal of tittering and pleasantry, he squeezed himself among them, and likened his condition to that of love among the roses. At this novel jest we all roared once more. "You should consider yourself highly honoured, sir," said we. "Sir," replied Mr Griggins, "you do me proud." Here everybody laughed again.

The tea-things having been removed, we all sat down to a round game, and here Mr Griggins shone forth with peculiar brilliancy. He made one most excellent joke in snuffing a candle, which was neither more nor less than setting fire to the hair of a pale young gentleman who sat next him, and afterwards begging his pardon with considerable humour. As the young gentleman could not see the joke, however, possibly in consequence of its being on the top of his own head, it did not go off quite as well as it might have done.

To recount all the drollery of Mr Griggins at supper would be impossible. How he drank out of other people's glasses, and ate of other people's bread, how he frightened into screaming convulsions a little boy who was sitting up to supper in a high chair, by sinking below the table and suddenly reappearing with a mask on; how the hostess was really surprised that anybody could find a pleasure in tormenting children, and how the host frowned at the hostess, and felt convinced that Mr Griggins had done it with the very best intentions; how Mr Griggins explained, and how everybody's good-humour was restored but the child's—to tell these and a hundred other things ever so briefly, would occupy more of our room and our reader's patience, than either they or we can conveniently spare.

Adapted from *The Funny Young Gentleman*, DICKENS.

As EXERCISES, the student should repeat his practice of all the excerpts given, in the light of the theoretical knowledge cumulatively acquired during the reading of this chapter.

CHAPTER 5

INTERPRETATION AND RENDERING

The technique of vocal expression has one general purpose only—that the communication of thought from speaker to listener shall be effective. Technique is the vehicle of expression; it must work smoothly and unobtrusively, and it must respond spontaneously to the changing demands of the sense under conveyance. The student will not be able to give his full concentration to his subject, his audience, the occasion, and to other matters demanding consideration, until his technique is flexible and largely automatic. It will then serve, and not restrict, his communication, and by its aid he will be able to express his thoughts and feelings accurately and sensitively.

Any form of oral reading is useful in consolidating the technique dealt with in the previous chapter, and also in developing sound methods of interpretation and presentation. Prose reading is, perhaps, the most useful form to begin with, as it is most closely identified with normal everyday speech activity. Verse-speaking has many uses in developing artistic speech, but verse should not be used to the exclusion of prose. The student must always guard against developing affectation of manner while concentrating upon literary and artistic forms which might differ from the style required by everyday speech, but which exercises, nevertheless, offer excellent practice material if treated sensibly. The student should, in any case, begin with, and constantly revert to, prose exercises, and should try to strike a happy medium between the utilitarian and the artistic.

The best way to approach the subject of oral prose reading is, firstly, to readjust the usual mental attitude by changing the description "reading aloud", by which this activity is frequently known. While attention is drawn to "reading", the speaker will not be sufficiently aware of the all-important necessity of communication. The following instructions, which give in detail the processes of comprehension and communication, should be applied consciously until they can be used habitually.

1. Glance at the excerpt in order to (a) note the subject, author, and any similar details; (b) note the general attitudes expressed and arguments developed; (c) form an opinion of the style of writing which may affect the style of rendering.
2. Absorb the sense of the first phrase.
3. Look at the audience (single or group, real or imaginary).
4. Focus your concentration on to the listener(s).
5. Speak (not read) the phrase to them.
6. Absorb the sense of the next phrase, and repeat the above sequence (3, 4 and 5), etc.

Consistent and regular exercise along these lines will reward the student by a "look and say" method of clear communication replacing the old "reading aloud" method which placed the emphasis on reading rather than on speaking. Naturally, the mechanical stage of this practice must not be carried too far; but sensibly approached, it will lead to (a) reduction of time taken for visual perception, (b) concentration on the interpretation of sense, (c) a more sharply defined focus of mental projection to the listener, resulting in (d) stronger communication of sense. Excerpts, suitable for this purpose, are not difficult to find, but the following is suggested for immediate practice.

It must not be imagined that a walking tour, as some would have us fancy, is merely a better or worse way of seeing the country. There are many ways of seeing a landscape quite as good; and none more vivid, in spite of canting dilettantes, than from a railway train. But landscape on a walking tour is quite accessory. He who is indeed of the brotherhood does not voyage in quest of the picturesque, but of certain jolly humours—of the hope and spirit with which the march begins at morning, and the peace and spiritual repletion of the evening's rest. He cannot tell whether he puts his knapsack on, or takes it off, with more delight. The excitement of the departure puts him in key for that of the arrival. Whatever he does is not only a reward in itself, but will be further rewarded in the sequel; and so pleasure leads on to pleasure in an endless chain. . . .

Now, to be properly enjoyed, a walking tour should be gone upon alone. If you go in a company, or even in pairs, it is no longer a walking tour in anything but name; it is something else and more in the nature of a picnic. A walking tour should be gone upon alone, because freedom is of the essence; because you should be able to stop and go on, and follow this way or that, as the freak takes you; and because you must have your own pace, and neither trot alongside a champion walker, nor mince in time with a girl. And then you must be open to all impressions and let your thoughts take colour from what you see. You should be as a pipe for any wind to play upon. "I cannot see the wit", says Hazlitt, "of walking and talking at the same time. When I am in the country I wish to vegetate like the country", which is the gist of all that can be said upon the matter. There should be no cackle of voices at your elbow, to jar on the meditative silence of the morning. And so long as a man is reasoning he cannot surrender himself to that fine intoxication that comes of much motion in the open air, that begins in a sort of dazzle and sluggishness of the brain, and ends in a peace that passes comprehension.

From *Walking Tours*, R. L. STEVENSON.

Further stimulus can be found by way of exercise in dramatic prose. The characterisation involved is found to intensify an otherwise dull manner of speech, especially if it is fully realised that the aim is not only to delineate character, but to project (at this stage by vocal means only) that character to the audience.

Sir Peter Teazle.

When an old bachelor marries a young wife, what is he to expect? 'Tis now six months since Lady Teazle made me the happiest of men—and I have been the most miserable dog ever since! We tift a little going to church, and fairly quarrelled before the bells had done ringing. I was more than once nearly choked with gall during the honeymoon, and had lost all comfort in life before my friends had done wishing me joy. Yet I chose with caution—a girl bred wholly in the country, who never knew luxury beyond one silk gown, nor dissipation above the annual gala of a race ball. Yet she now plays her part in all the extravagant fopperies of fashion and town, with as ready a grace as if she never had seen a bush or a grass-plot out of Grosvenor Square! I am sneered at by all my acquaintance, and paragraphed in the newspapers. She dissipates my fortune, and contradicts all my humours; yet the worst of it is, I doubt I love her, or I should never bear all this. However, I'll never be weak enough to own it.

From *The School for Scandal*, SHERIDAN.

Mirabell.

. . . Well, have I liberty to offer conditions—That when you are dwindled into a wife, I may not be beyond measure enlarged into a husband? . . . I thank you. Imprimis, then, I covenant that your acquaintance be general; that you admit no sworn confidant, or intimate of your own sex; no she-friend to screen her affairs under your countenance, and tempt you to make trial of a mutual secrecy. No decoy duck to wheedle you a fop-scrambling to the play in a mask—Then bring you home in a pretended fright, when you think you shall be found out—And rail at me for missing the play and disappointing the frolic which you had to pick me up and prove my constancy. . . . Item, I article that you continue to like your own face as long as I shall: and while it passes current with me, that you endeavour not to new coin it. To which end, together with all vizards for the day, I prohibit all masks for the night, made of oiled skins and I know not what—hog's bones, hare's gall, and the marrow of a roasted cat. In short, I forbid all commerce with the gentlewoman in what-d'ye-call-it Court. Lastly, to the dominion of the tea-table I submit—but with proviso, that you exceed not in your province; but restrain yourself to native and simple tea-table drinks, as tea, chocolate, and coffee. As likewise to genuine and authorized tea-table talk—such as mending of fashions, spoiling reputations, railing at absent friends, and so forth—but that on no account you encroach upon the men's prerogative, and presume to drink healths or toast fellows; for prevention of which I banish all foreign forces, all auxilliaries to the tea-table, as orange-brandy, all aniseed, cinnamon, citron, and Barbadoes waters, together with ratafia, and the most noble spirit of Clary. But for cowslip-wine, poppy-water, and all dormatives, those I allow. These provisos admitted, in other things I may prove a tractable and complying husband.

From *The Way of the World*, CONGREVE.

Rosalind.

It is not the fashion to see the lady the epilogue; but it is no more unhandsome than to see the lord the prologue. If it be true that good wine needs no bush, 'tis true that a good play needs no epilogue: yet to good wine they do use good bushes; and good plays prove the better by the help of good epilogues. What a case am I in then, that am neither a good epilogue, nor cannot insinuate with you in the behalf of a good play? I am not furnished like a beggar, therefore to beg will not become me: my way is to conjure you; and I'll begin with the women. I charge you, O women, for the love you bear to men, to like as much of this play as please them: and so I charge you, O men, for the love you bear to women (as I perceive by your simpering, none of you hate them), that between you and the women the play may please. If I were a woman, I would kiss as many of you as had beards that pleased me, complexions that liked me and breaths that I defied not: and, I am sure, as many as have good beards or good faces or sweet breaths will, for my kind offer, when I make my curtsy, bid me farewell.

From *As You Like It*, SHAKESPEARE.

In verse-speaking, the technique becomes rather more involved, for the sense-content is expressed through a rhythmic pattern. The verse-speaker is confronted with the problem of conveying the meaning and of establishing the rhythmic shape of the verse at one and the same time. Moreover, he must communicate the meaning intended by the poet and re-create the rhythmic pattern with such perfect balance that sense will not blatantly destroy the rhythmic qualities, nor yet the rhythm by becoming "metrical", obscure the sense-content by which the poetic imagery is manifested.

It is of primary importance that the reader should be able to recognise the basic rhythm of a poem. Rhythm is the result of stress pattern (as explained on page 47), and its analysis is called scansion. Generally speaking, there are two ways in which this matter is approached. One method is to mark each syllable to indicate whether it is relatively light or heavy, so that the markings will indicate visually a preponderance of a particular basic unit (called a "foot"), from which the metre, *i.e.* the measurement of the rhythm, may be ascertained. This method might be used by a student with little or no natural sense of rhythm, but it is certainly not recommended for practical verse-speaking.

The method advocated in connection with speech training is that of reading the poem through, as "sensibly" as possible, allowing the rhythm to reveal itself. In all good verse there is so perfect a marriage between sound and sense, between music and meaning, that, with perhaps a little assistance from the tutor, the student should be able to recognise instinctively the basic rhythm with which he is dealing. This is by far the better method. Too much analytical scansion can, and frequently does, impede rhythmic flow by metrical consciousness, and at times might even obscure meaning by mechanically adjusted stresses.

Our commonest rhythm is based on the iambic foot, *i.e.* on a foot of two syllables (dissyllabic), the first a light and the second a heavy beat, as in the words, "ăbōve" and "ăroūnd". It should be noticed that in continuous speech the feet and the words do not correspond, for example, "Fŏr onсe,| ŭpōn| ă rāw| aňd gūs|tў dāy." In the following example the basic rhythm will have revealed itself as iambic before the student will have read (aloud) many lines.

> Bid me to live, and I will live,
>   Thy Protestant to be:
> Or bid me love, and I will give
>   A loving heart to thee.
>
> A heart as soft, a heart as kind,
>   A heart as sound and free
> As in the whole world thou canst find,
>   That heart I'll give to thee.
>
> Bid that heart stay, and it will stay,
>   To honour thy decree:
> Or bid it languish quite away,
>   And't shall do so for thee.

Bid me to weep, and I will weep
   While I have eyes to see:
And having none, yet I will keep
   A heart to weep for thee.

Bid me despair, and I'll despair,
   Under that cypress tree:
Or bid me die, and I will dare
   E'en Death, to die for thee.

Thou art my life, my love, my heart,
   The very eyes of me,
And hast command of every part,
   To live and die for thee.

                    To Anthea, HERRICK.

The trochaic foot, the reverse of the iambic, is also dissyllabic, but with the stress on the first syllable, and is the basic foot used in the following poem.

Hail to thee, blithe Spirit!
   Bird thou never wert,
That from Heaven, or near it,
   Pourest thy full heart
In profuse strains of unpremeditated art.

Higher still and higher
   From the earth thou springest
Like a cloud of fire;
   The blue deep thou wingest,
And singing still dost soar, and soaring ever singest.

In the golden lightning
   Of the sunken sun,
O'er which clouds are bright'ning,
   Thou dost float and run;
Like an unbodied joy whose race is just begun.

The pale purple even
    Melts around thy flight;
Like a star of Heaven,
    In the broad daylight
Thou art unseen, but yet I hear thy shrill delight.

Keen as are the arrows
    Of that silver sphere,
Whose intense lamp narrows
    In the white dawn clear
Until we hardly see—we feel that it is there.

All the earth and air
    With thy voice is loud,
As, when night is bare,
    From one lonely cloud
The moon rains out her beams, and Heaven is
    overflowed.

What thou art we know not;
    What is most like thee?
From rainbow clouds there flow not
    Drops so bright to see
As from thy presence showers a rain of melody.

Like a Poet hidden
    In a light of thought,
Singing hymns unbidden,
    Till the world is wrought
To sympathy with hopes and fears it heeded not:

Like a high-born maiden
    In a palace tower,
Soothing her love-laden
    Soul in secret hour
With music sweet as love, which overflows her bower:

Like a glow-worm golden
  In a dell of dew,
Scattering unbeholden
  Its aëreal hue
Among the flowers and grass, which screen it from
    the view!

Like a rose embowered
  In its own green leaves,
By warm winds deflowered,
  Till the scent it gives
Makes faint with too much sweet those heavy wingèd
    thieves:

Sound of vernal showers
  On the twinkling grass,
Rain-awakened flowers,
  All that ever was
Joyous, and clear, and fresh, thy music doth surpass:

Teach us, Sprite or Bird,
  What sweet thoughts are thine:
I have never heard
  Praise of love or wine
That panted forth a flood of rapture so divine.

Chorus Hymeneal,
  Or triumphal chant,
Marched with thine would be all
  But an empty vaunt,
A thing wherein we feel there is some hidden want.

What objects are the fountains
  Of thy happy strain?
What fields, or waves, or mountains?
  What shapes of sky or plain?
What love of thine own kind? what ignorance of pain?

With thy clear keen joyance
   Languor cannot be:
Shadow of annoyance
   Never came near thee:
Thou lovest—but ne'er knew love's sad satiety.

Waking or asleep,
   Thou of death must deem
Things more true and deep
   Than we mortals dream,
Or how could thy notes flow in such a crystal stream?

We look before and after,
   And pine for what is not:
Our sincerest laughter
   With some pain is fraught;
Our sweetest songs are those that tell of saddest thoughts.

Yet if we could scorn
   Hate, and pride, and fear;
If we were things born
   Not to shed a tear,
I know not how thy joy we ever should come near.

Better than all measures
   Of delightful sound,
Better than all treasures
   That in books are found,
Thy skill to poet were, thou scorner of the ground!

Teach me half the gladness
   That thy brain must know,
Such harmonious madness
   From my lips would flow
The world should listen then—as I am listening now.

To a Skylark, SHELLEY.

The anapæst is a foot of three syllables, with the stress on the third. It is quite clearly the basis of the rhythm of the next example.

The Assyrian came down like the wolf on the fold,
And his cohorts were gleaming in purple and gold;
And the sheen of their spears was like stars on the sea,
When the blue wave rolls nightly in deep Galilee.

Like the leaves of the forest when Summer is green,
That host with their banners at sunset were seen;
Like the leaves of the forest when Autumn hath blown,
That host on the morrow lay wither'd and strown.

For the Angel of Death spread his wings on the blast,
And breathed in the face of the foe as he pass'd:
And the eyes of the sleepers wax'd deadly and chill,
And their hearts but once heaved, and for ever grew still!

And there lay the steed with his nostril all wide,
But through it there rolled not the breath of his pride;
And the foam of his gasping lay white on the turf,
And cold as the spray of the rock-beating surf.

And there lay the rider distorted and pale,
With the dew on his brow, and the rust on his mail:
And the tents were all silent, the banners alone,
The lances unlifted, the trumpet unblown.

And the widows of Ashur are loud in their wail,
And the idols are broke in the temple of Baal;
And the might of the Gentile, unsmote by the sword,
Hath melted like snow in the glance of the Lord!

The Destruction of Sennacherib, BYRON.

The reverse of anapæstic metre is dactylic. The dactyl, being also trisyllabic but with the stress on the first syllable, is found in many English words, such as "faithfully" and "blundering". In continuous speech, however, the dactylic tends to become anapæstic, except in poems of short lines, where the duration is too short for this tendency to develop, as in the next example.

> One more Unfortunate,
>   Weary of breath,
> Rashly importunate,
>   Gone to her death!
>
> Take her up tenderly,
>   Lift her with care;
> Fashion'd so slenderly,
>   Young, and so fair!
>
> Look at her garments
> Clinging like cerements;
> Whilst the wave constantly
>   Drips from her clothing;
> Take her up instantly,
>   Loving, not loathing.
>
> Touch her not scornfully;
> Think of her mournfully,
>   Gently and humanly;
> Not of the stains of her,
> All that remains of her
>   Now is pure womanly.
>
> Make no deep scrutiny
> Into her mutiny
>   Rash and undutiful:
> Past all dishonour,
> Death has left on her
>   Only the beautiful.

Still, for all slips of hers,
One of Eve's family—
Wipe those poor lips of hers
Oozing so clammily.

Loop up her tresses
Escaped from the comb,
Her fair auburn tresses;
Whilst wonderment guesses
Where was her home?

Who was her father?
Who was her mother?
Had she a sister?
Had she a brother?
Or was there a dearer one
Still, and a nearer one
Yet, than all other?

Alas! for the rarity
Of Christian charity
Under the sun!
O, it was pitiful!
Near a whole city full,
Home she had none.

Sisterly, brotherly,
Fatherly, motherly,
Feelings had changed:
Love, by harsh evidence,
Thrown from its eminence;
Even God's providence
Seeming estranged.

G

Where the lamps quiver
So far in the river,
  With many a light
From window and casement,
From garret to basement,
She stood, with amazement,
  Houseless by night.

The bleak wind of March
  Made her tremble and shiver;
But not the dark arch,
  Or the black flowing river:
Mad from life's history,
Glad to death's mystery,
  Swift to be hurl'd—
Anywhere, anywhere
  Out of the world!

In she plunged boldly—
No matter how coldly
  The rough river ran—
Over the brink of it,
Picture it—think of it,
  Dissolute Man!
Lave in it, drink of it,
  Then, if you can!

Take her up tenderly,
  Lift her with care;
Fashion'd so slenderly,
  Young, and so fair!

Ere her limbs frigidly
Stiffen too rigidly,
  Decently, kindly,
Smooth and compose them,
And her eyes, close them,
  Staring so blindly!

Dreadfully staring
  Thro' muddy impurity,
As when with the daring
Last look of despairing
  Fix'd on futurity.

Perishing gloomily,
Spurr'd by contumely,
Cold inhumanity,
Burning insanity,
  Into her rest.—
Cross her hands humbly
As if praying dumbly,
  Over her breast!

Owning her weakness,
  Her evil behaviour,
And leaving, with meekness,
  Her sins to her Saviour!

The Bridge of Sighs, HOOD.

Similarly with amphibrachic metre, of which the basis is a heavy syllable, preceded and followed by light syllables (as in "cŏnsū̄mmaťe" and "tŏgē̄thĕr"), there is a tendency towards confusion, in actual verse speaking, with anapæstic metre, as in the example on the following pages.

It must be clearly understood that the metrical foot is only the basis of verse structure, and its nature is best ascertained as the result of the rhythm having been instinctively recognised during an expressive rendering. There are a great many metrical irregularities, such as substitutions and inversions, to be observed in poetry, frequently resulting in an effect desired, consciously or unconsciously, by the poet. Over-meticulous analysis of the irregularities of metre is not likely to lead to sensitive verse-speaking. Rhythm should be felt; it need not be metrically understood. The student must realise that rhythm is the principal means whereby the poet expresses his emotion in verse form, and that in the rendering of verse a knowledge of metre is not synonymous with a sense of rhythmic perception.

One single example will suffice to support the attitude just expressed. In the following poem, an analysis of the first several lines would seem to indicate an amphibrachic intention:

I sprang to | the stirrup, | and Joris, | and he;
I galloped, Dirck galloped, we galloped all three;
"Good speed!" cried the watch, as the gate bolts
    undrew;

whereas a sensitive reading of the whole poem suggests an anapæstic intention, borne out subsequently by—

Not a word | to each oth|er; we kept | the great pace |
Neck by neck, stride by stride, never changing our place.

This is not merely of academic interest; it is of great practical value. The amphibrachic metre, if accepted as the basic metre of the entire poem, would suggest only a mild canter, whereas the anapæstic metre forms the basis of a rhythm much more suggestive of the atmosphere of the desperate gallop.

I sprang to the stirrup, and Joris, and he;
I galloped, Dirck galloped, we galloped all three;
"Good speed!" cried the watch, as the gate bolts undrew;
"Speed!" echoed the wall to us galloping through;
Behind shut the postern, the light sank to rest,
And into the midnight we galloped abreast.

Not a word to each other; we kept the great pace
Neck by neck, stride by stride, never changing our place;
I turned in my saddle and made its girths tight,
Then shortened each stirrup, and set the pique right,
Rebuckled the cheek-strap, chained slacker the bit,
Nor galloped less steadily Roland a whit.

'Twas moonset at starting; but while we drew near
Lokeren, the cocks crew and twilight dawned clear;
At Boom, a great yellow star came out to see;
At Düffeld, 'twas morning as plain as could be;
And from Mechlen church-steeple we heard the half chime,
So, Joris broke silence with "Yet there is time!"

At Aeshot, up leaped of a sudden the sun,
And against him the cattle stood black every one,
To stare thro' the mist at us galloping past,
And I saw my stout galloper Roland at last,
With resolute shoulders, each butting away
The haze, as some bluff river headland its spray:

And his low head and crest, just one sharp ear bent back
For my voice, and the other pricked out on his track;
And one eye's black intelligence—ever that glance
O'er its white edge at me, his own master, askance!
And the thick heavy spume-flakes which aye and anon
His fierce lips shook upwards in galloping on.

By Hasselt, Dirck groaned; and cried Joris, "Stay spur!
Your Roos galloped bravely, the fault's not in her,
We'll remember at Aix"—for one heard the quick wheeze
Of her chest, saw the stretched neck and staggering knees,
And sunk tail, and horrible heave of the flank,
As down on her haunches she shuddered and sank.

So we were left galloping, Joris and I,
Past Looz and past Tongres, no cloud in the sky;
The broad sun above laughed a pitiless laugh,
'Neath our feet broke the brittle bright stubble like chaff;
Till over by Dalhem a dome-spire sprang white,
And "Gallop," gasped Joris, "for Aix is in sight!

How they'll greet us!" and all in a moment his roan
Rolled neck and croup over, lay dead as a stone;
And there was my Roland to bear the whole weight
Of the news which alone would save Aix from her fate,
With his nostrils like pits full of blood to the brim,
And with circles of red for his eye-sockets' rim.

Then I cast loose my buffcoat, each holster let fall,
Shook off both my jack-boots, let go belt and all,
Stood up in the stirrup, leaned, patted his ear,
Called my Roland his pet-name, my horse without peer;
Clapped my hands, laughed and sang, any noise, bad or
    good,
Till at length into Aix Roland galloped and stood.

And all I remember is, friends flocking round
As I sat with his head 'twixt my knees on the ground,
And no voice but was praising this Roland of mine,
As I poured down this throat our last measure of wine,
Which (the burgesses voted by common consent)
Was no more than his due who brought good news from Ghent.

> *How They Brought the Good News From Ghent to Aix.*
>   ROBERT BROWNING.

Should the student be interested in enlarging his
knowledge of prosody and versification, he is recommended
to study the subject in the appropriate books listed in the
bibliography. He should be warned, however, that the
best poetry will always defy complete analysis, whilst
for FREE VERSE, and for poems using SPRUNG RHYTHM, the
metrical foot basis is of little or no practical use whatso-
ever. Figures of speech, and such devices as onomatopœia,
should be known by the student, but when encountered in
verse they should not be consciously underlined but
should be allowed to create their own effect.

In addition to rhythmic flow, verse also has form.

The verse speaker must establish the pattern of the verse so that it is perceived as definitely by the ear of the listener, as it is recognised visually by the reader.

The sentences, conveying meaning, very rarely coincide with the arrangement of lines which are mainly responsible for pattern. By way of experiment it is suggested that the following exercise is read with the intention of establishing the meaning only.

I stood tiptoe upon a little hill, the air was cooling and so very still that the sweet buds, which with a modest pride pull droopingly, in slanting curve aside, their scantly leaved and finely tapering stems, had not yet lost those starry diadems caught from the early sobbing of the morn.

The clouds were pure and white as flocks new shorn and, fresh from the clear brook, sweetly they slept on the blue fields of heaven, and then there crept a little noiseless noise among the leaves, born of the very sigh that silence heaves. For not the faintest motion could be seen of all the shades that slanted o'er the green.

There was wide wandering for the greediest eye to peer about upon variety far around the horizon's crystal air to skim, and trace the dwindled edgings of its brim to picture out the quaint and curious bending of a fresh woodland alley, never ending, or by the bowery clefts and leafy shelves guess where the jaunty streams refresh themselves.

I gazed awhile, and felt as light, and free as though the fanning wings of Mercury had played upon my heels. I was light-hearted, and many pleasures to my vision started, so I straightway began to pluck a posey of luxuries bright, milky, soft and rosy.

To any but the least sensitive reader, the poetic thought, language and rhythm of the above excerpt will have made itself felt. Yet it was not verse. It lacked a satisfying and appropriate pattern. A further experiment, attempting to establish pattern by itself is worth trying, especially as a line-by-line rendering is one of the commonest faults in early attempts at verse-reading. It will be quite clear that pattern by itself cannot be relied upon.

> I stood tiptoe upon a little hill.
> The air was cooling, and so very still.
> That the sweet buds, which with a modest pride.
> Pull droopingly, in slanting curve aside.
> Their scantly leav'd, and finely tapering stems.
> Had not yet lost those starry diadems.
> Caught from the early sobbing of the morn.

Reading the above short excerpt, with a falling inflection to mark the completion of each line in an attempt to enforce a pattern, will have seriously interrupted the fluency of the sense-content, and will have rendered all rhythmical continuity impossible.

By now it will be quite clear that some compromise arrangement will have to be made in order to satisfy the demands of sense, rhythmic continuity and verse pattern, and to achieve this the ends of the lines require special treatment. An examination of the poem, now to be given in its correct form, will reveal that only in three lines is the sense concluded at the line-end. The other lines have, to a greater or lesser extent, an overflow of sense into the next line; they are enjambed lines, and they require to be treated with a SUSPENSORY PAUSE in order to satisfy the joint demands of meaning and pattern. This "pause" is applied *on* a word, rather than *between* words; although it has the effect of a pause, it is in reality a suspension of pace and pitch on the last syllable of an enjambed line. It indicates the end of the verse line, and it gives an impression of initial attack (without actual force) at the beginning of the following line; moreover, it has these effects without interrupting the sense. The complete poem should now be attempted.

I stood tiptoe upon a little hill,
The air was cooling, and so very still,
That the sweet buds which with a modest pride
Pull droopingly, in slanting curve aside,
Their scantly leav'd and finely tapering stems,
Had not yet lost those starry diadems
Caught from the early sobbing of the morn.
The clouds were pure and white as flocks new shorn,
And fresh from the clear brook; sweetly they slept
On the blue fields of heaven, and then there crept
A little noiseless noise among the leaves,
Born of the very sigh that silence heaves:
For not the faintest motion could be seen
Of all the shades that slanted o'er the green.
There was wide wand'ring for the greediest eye,
To peer about upon variety;
Far around the horizon's crystal air to skim,
And trace the dwindled edgings of its brim;
To picture out the quaint, and curious bending
Of a fresh woodland alley, never ending;
Or by the bowery clefts, and leafy shelves,
Guess where the jaunty streams refresh themselves.
I gazed awhile, and felt as light, and free
As though the fanning wings of Mercury
Had played upon my heels: I was light-hearted,
And many pleasures to my vision started;
So I straightway began to pluck a posey
Of luxuries bright, milky, soft and rosy.

I Stood Tiptoe, KEATS.

The reading of a long poem might still become some-what monotonous in its technique were it not for the use of the CÆSURA, a pause which occurs *during* a line of verse and not necessarily marked by punctuation. It usually follows the strongest word of the line, and it creates, as it were, variety of rhythmic balance within the more regular quantity of the complete line. In the following excerpt the position of the early cæsural pauses are indicated, and it will be found that the fairly regular iambic pentameter is delicately relieved by the balanced variety which causes the first six lines to have a more interesting grouping of 3, 2, 1, 4, 3, 2, 3, 2, 3, 2, 2, 3, as a subtle undercurrent to the more obvious 5, 5, 5, 5, 5, 5.

Portia.

> The quality of mercy/is not strain'd;
> It droppeth,/as the gentle rain from heaven
> Upon the place beneath:/ it is twice bless'd;
> It blesseth him that gives/and him that takes:
> 'Tis mightiest in the mightiest;/it becomes
> The thronèd monarch/better than his crown:
> His sceptre shows the force of temporal power,
> The attribute to awe and majesty,
> Wherein doth sit the dread and fear of kings;
> But mercy is above this sceptred sway;
> It is enthronèd in the hearts of kings,
> It is an attribute to God himself;
> And earthly power doth then shew likest God's,
> When mercy seasons justice. Therefore, Jew,
> Though justice be thy plea, consider this—
> That, in the course of justice, none of us
> Should see salvation: we do pray for mercy;
> And that same prayer doth teach us all to render
> The deeds of mercy. I have spoke thus much
> To mitigate the justice of thy plea;
> Which if thou follow, this strict court of Venice
> Must needs give sentence 'gainst the merchant there.

From *The Merchant of Venice*, SHAKESPEARE.

A verse speaker should be able to recognise stanza form, a pattern unit consisting of a set of lines grouped together within a poem, and to mark them artistically during a rendering. At times, a stanza, finishing with an incomplete thought, needs an extended suspensory pause and very careful inflectional control, as at the end of the second, third, seventh, eighth and ninth stanzas of the following poem.

I

O Wild West Wind, thou breath of Autumn's being,
Thou, from whose unseen presence the leaves dead
Are driven, like ghosts from an enchanter fleeing,

Yellow, and black, and pale, and hectic red,
Pestilence-stricken multitudes!   O thou,
Who chariotest to their dark wintry bed

The wingèd seeds, where they lie cold and low,
Each like a corpse within its grave, until
Thine azure sister of the Spring shall blow

Her clarion o'er the dreaming earth, and fill
(Driving sweet buds like flocks to feed in air)
With living hues and odours plain and hill:

Wild Spirit, which art moving everywhere;
Destroyer and preserver; hear, oh, hear!

II

Thou on whose stream, 'mid the steep sky's commotion,
Loose clouds like earth's decaying leaves are shed,
Shook from the tangled boughs of Heaven and Ocean,

Angels of rain and lightning: there are spread
On the blue surface of thine aery surge,
Like the bright hair uplifted from the head

Of some fierce Mænad, even from the dim verge
Of the horizon to the zenith's height,
The locks of the approaching storm.   Thou dirge

Of the dying year, to which this closing night
Will be the dome of a vast sepulchre,
Vaulted with all thy congregated might

Of vapours, from whose solid atmosphere
Black rain, and fire, and hail will burst: oh, hear!

III

Thou who didst waken from his summer dreams
The blue Mediterranean, where he lay,
Lulled by the coil of his crystalline streams,

Beside a pumice isle in Baiae's bay,
And saw in sleep old palaces and towers
Quivering within the wave's intenser day,

All overgrown with azure moss and flowers
So sweet, the sense faints picturing them!   Thou
For whose path the Atlantic's level powers

Cleave themselves into chasms, while far below
The sea-blooms and the oozy woods which wear
The sapless foliage of the ocean, know

Thy voice, and suddenly grow gray with fear,
And tremble and despoil themselves: oh, hear!

IV

If I were a dead leaf thou mightest bear;
If I were a swift cloud to fly with thee;
A wave to pant beneath thy power, and share

The impulse of thy strength, only less free
Than thou, O uncontrollable!   If even
I were as in my boyhood, and could be

The comrade of thy wanderings over Heaven,
As then, when to outstrip thy skiey speed
Scarce seemed a vision; I would ne'er have striven

As thus with thee in prayer in my sore need.
Oh, lift me as a wave, a leaf, a cloud!
I fall upon the thorns of life! I bleed!

A heavy weight of hours has chained and bowed
One too like thee: tameless, and swift, and proud.

V

Make me thy lyre, even as the forest is:
What if my leaves are falling like its own!
The tumult of thy mighty harmonies

Will take from both a deep, autumnal tone,
Sweet though in sadness.   Be thou, Spirit fierce,
My spirit!   Be thou me, impetuous one!

Drive my dead thoughts over the universe
Like withered leaves to quicken a new birth!
And, by the incantation of this verse,

Scatter, as from an unextinguished hearth
Ashes and sparks, my words among mankind!
Be through my lips to unawakened earth

The trumpet of a prophecy!   O Wind,
If Winter comes, can Spring be far behind?

Ode to the West Wind, SHELLEY.

It is desirable that a verse speaker should be able to recognise the various conventional stanza forms used in English verse, but a detailed description of them is not within the scope of this book. The SONNET, however, needs special mention, as its compressed unity of thought, and the structure of its metrical form, cause it to be the supreme test of a verse speaker's capabilities.

There are two sonnet forms used in English poetry. Both have fourteen lines each of five iambic feet. The Italian form is divided into two parts, the first eight lines forming an octet, and the remaining six, the sestet, clearly shown in—

> Farewell, Love! and all thy laws for ever;
>   Thy baited hooks shall tangle me no more.
>   Senec and Plato call me from thy lore
>   To perfect wealth my wit for to endeavour.
> In blind errour when I did persèver,
>   Thy sharp repulse, that pricketh aye so sore,
>   Taught me in trifles that I set no store,
> But scape forth thence, since liberty is lever.
>   Therefore, farewell! go, trouble younger hearts,
>   And in me claim no more authority.
>   With idle youth go use thy property,
>   And thereon spend thy many brittle darts;
>   For hitherto, though I have lost my time,
>   Me list no longer rotten boughs to clime.
>
> *A Renouncing of Love*, SIR THOMAS WYATT.

It will have been noticed from the above sonnet, that the clear rhyming scheme enforces the strict unity of the theme, and also clearly identifies the octet and the sestet respectively.

Milton varied the Italian model by smoothly linking the octet and the sestet, improving the continuity without undermining the development or lessening the effect of the climax. The rhyming scheme, a b b a a b b a c d c d c d, clearly marks the octet and sestet separately, but the enjambment linking the eighth to the ninth line should be noticed in the following example:

> Avenge, O Lord, thy slaughtered saints, whose bones
>   Lie scattered on the Alpine mountains cold;
>   Even them who kept thy truth so pure of old,
>   When all our fathers worshipped stocks and stones,
> Forget not: in thy book record their groans
>   Who were thy sheep, and in their ancient fold
>   Slain by the bloody Piedmontese, that rolled
>   Mother with infant down the rocks.   Their moans
> The vales redoubled to the hills, and they
>   To Heaven.   Their martyred blood and ashes sow
>   O'er all th' Italian fields, where still doth sway
> The triple Tyrant; that from these may grow
>   A hundredfold, who, having learnt thy way,
>   Early may fly the Babylonian woe.

> *On the Late Massacre in Piedmont*, MILTON.

A Shakespearean sonnet consists of three quatrains (groups of four lines) and a couplet. The rhyming scheme, a b a b c d c d e f e f g g, assists a more steady climax through the entire poem, culminating in the final couplet. Nevertheless, there is still the suggestion of change of thought and mood with the ninth line as in the earlier forms.

> Shall I compare thee to a summer's day?
> Thou art more lovely and more temperate;
> Rough winds do shake the darling buds of May,
> And summer's lease hath all too short a date:
> Sometimes too hot the eye of heaven shines,
> And often is his gold complexion dimm'd:
> And every fair to fair sometime declines,
> By chance, or nature's changing course, untrimm'd:

But thy eternal summer shall not fade
Nor lose possession of that fair thou owest;
Nor shall Death brag thou wanderest in his shade
When in eternal lines to time thou growest.
So long as men can breathe, or eyes can see
So long lives this, and this gives life to thee.

Sonnet No. 18, SHAKESPEARE.

Free verse was mentioned earlier. It is written either
with several intermingling metres or with no metre. Its
characteristic is lack of rhyming scheme, and of form,
giving complete freedom from metrical pattern. Its
effect is the result of using rhythmical sense-cadences
rather than metrical feet as its basis. In rendering free
verse, the ability to unobtrusively change the rhythm to
indicate the poet's fluctuating mood is most essential.

Hark, ah, the nightingale—
The tawny-throated!
Hark, from that moonlit cedar what a burst!
What triumph! hark!—what pain!

O wanderer from a Grecian shore,
Still, after many years, in distant lands,
Still nourishing in thy bewilder'd brain
That wild, unquench'd, deep-sunken, old-world pain—
Say, will it never heal?
And can this fragrant lawn
With its cool trees, and night,
And the sweet, tranquil Thames,
And moonshine, and the dew,
To thy rack'd heart and brain
Afford no balm?

Dost thou to-night behold,
Here, through the moonlight on this English grass,
The unfriendly palace in the Thracian wild?
Dost thou again peruse
With hot cheeks and sear'd eyes
The too clear web, and thy dumb sister's shame?
Dost thou once more assay
Thy flight, and feel come over thee,
Poor fugitive, the feathery change
Once more, and once more seem to make resound
With love and hate, triumph and agony,
Lone Daulis, and the high Cephissian vale?
Listen, Eugenia—
How thick the bursts come crowding through the leaves!
Again—thou hearest?
Eternal passion!
Eternal pain!

Philomela, MATTHEW ARNOLD.

In the field of poetry there are two principal, and easily
recognised, classes. Poetry through which a writer
expresses his own feelings is called LYRICAL poetry.
NON-LYRICAL verse may describe scenes, it may narrate
events, or it may even portray a character by using the
direct speech of a real or imaginary person.

True lyrics are always short and intense in feeling.
Being subjective in nature, the thought expressed is also
necessarily compressed. Sometimes a lyric appears to be
descriptive and therefore non-lyrical, because the poet may
be able to express his mood only by describing a certain
experience. Provided he has expressed his mood, the
poem will be lyrical.

This introspective, and frequently retrospective, nature
of lyrical poetry, demands of the verse speaker an appropriate manner of rendering. Absolute repose physically,
sensitive understanding of the poet's emotion, and an
identification of the speaker's mood with that of the poet.

H

Technically, emphasis is obtained by the use of compound inflections to soften the normal sense-stresses, and there must be the smoothest continuity of rhythm. The feeling must be so strong, but so restrained in its expression, and the technique must be so unobtrusive in its application, that the resultant communication will give the impression of thought projection, rather than audible "verse-speaking". Consider this advice, and concentrate well on the feeling of the following lyric, before attempting to speak it.

Come to me in the silence of the night;
   Come in the speaking silence of a dream;
Come with soft rounded cheeks and eyes as bright
   As sunlight on a stream;
     Come back in tears,
O memory, hope and love of finished years.

O dream how sweet, too sweet, too bitter-sweet,
   Whose wakening should have been in Paradise,
Where souls brim-full of love abide and meet;
   Where thirsting longing eyes
     Watch the slow door
That opening, letting in, lets out no more.

Yet come to me in dreams, that I may live
   My very life again though cold in death;
Come back to me in dreams, that I may give
   Pulse for pulse, breath for breath:
     Speak low, lean low,
As long ago, my love, how long ago.

Echo, CHRISTINA ROSSETTI.

Also, in a descriptive style, the poet may clearly express a mood through a scene as in the following poem which naturally demands a quiet subjective manner.

The sheep-bell tolleth curfew-time;
   The gnats, a busy rout,
Fleck the warm air; the dismal owl
   Shouteth a sleepy shout;
The voiceless bat, more felt than seen,
   Is flitting round about.

The aspen leaflets scarcely stir;
   The river seems to think;
Athwart the dusk, broad primroses
   Look coldly from the brink,
Where, listening to the freshet's noise,
   The quiet cattle drink.

The bees boom past; the white moths rise
   Like spirits from the ground;
The gray flies hum their weary tune,
   A distant, dream-like sound;
And far, far off, to the slumb'rous eve,
   Bayeth an old guardhound.

An Evening Scene, COVENTRY PATMORE.

A poet may, of course, express the feelings of another person in direct speech, as in a soliloquy through a character other than his own. In such poems the thought is still the dominant factor, and such poems are best not "characterised". Somewhere, however, the border-line must be crossed from lyrical to non-lyrical verse, and of the latter the next selection is representative of NARRATIVE verse. In this kind of verse the telling of the story must be the primary concern of the speaker, and it is better if the rendering remains vocal and not physical in expression. The dramatic action suggested in the script will be much more vivid in the minds of the listeners if the poem is spoken convincingly. Gestures are more likely to distract than to stimulate the imagination of the audience.

The rain set early in to-night,
  The sullen wind was soon awake,
It tore the elm-tops down for spite,
  And did its worst to vex the lake,
  I listened with heart fit to break.

When glided in Porphyria; straight
  She shut the cold out and the storm,
And kneeled and made the cheerless grate
  Blaze up, and all the cottage warm;
  Which done, she rose, and from her form

Withdrew the dripping cloak and shawl,
  And laid her soiled gloves by, untied
Her hat and let the damp hair fall,
  And last, she sat down by my side
  And called me. When no voice replied,

She put my arm about her waist,
  And made her smooth white shoulder bare,
And all her yellow hair displaced,
  And, stooping, made my cheek lie there,
  And spread, o'er all, her yellow hair—

Murmuring how she loved me—she,
  Too weak, for all her heart's endeavour,
To set its struggling passion free
  From pride, and vainer ties dissever,
  And give herself to me for ever.

But passion sometimes would prevail,
  Nor could to-night's gay feast restrain
A sudden thought of one so pale
  For love of her, and all in vain:
  So, she was come through wind and rain.

Be sure I looked up at her eyes
   Happy and proud; at last I knew
Porphyria worshipped me; surprise
   Made my heart swell, and still it grew
   While I debated what to do.

That moment she was mine, mine, fair,
   Perfectly pure and good: I found
A thing to do, and all her hair
   In one long yellow string I wound
   Three times her little throat around,

And strangled her.   No pain felt she;
   I am quite sure she felt no pain.
As a shut bud that holds a bee,
   I warily oped her lids; again
   Laughed the blue eyes without a stain.

And I untightened next the tress
   About her neck; her cheek once more
Blushed bright beneath my burning kiss:
   I propped her head up as before.
   Only, this time my shoulder bore

Her head, which droops upon it still:
   The smiling rosy little head,
So glad it has its utmost will,
   That all it scorned at once is fled,
   And I, its love, am gained instead

Porphyria's love: she guessed not how
   Her darling one wish would be heard.
And thus we sit together now,
   And all night long we have not stirred,
   And yet God has not said a word!

              Porphyria's Lover, ROBERT BROWNING.

DRAMATIC VERSE involves physical characterisation which, strictly speaking, does not come within the scope of "Speech Training". There are, however, many passages, especially from Shakespeare, in which the thought is subjective. Such passages are usually given a lyrical treatment vocally, even during a dramatic performance of the entire play, the actor temporarily submerging the physical in the mental. Such passages as the following offer suitable practice.

Juliet.

> Shall I speak ill of him that is my husband?
> Ah, poor my lord, what tongue shall smooth thy name,
> When I, thy three-hours' wife, have mangled it?—
> But wherefore, villain, didst thou kill my cousin?
> That villain cousin would have kill'd my husband:
> Back, foolish tears, back to your native spring;
> Your tributary drops belong to woe,
> Which you, mistaking, offer up to joy.
> My husband lives, that Tybalt would have slain;
> And Tybalt's dead, that would have slain my husband:
> All this is comfort; wherefore weep I then?
> Some word there was, worser than Tybalt's death,
> That murder'd me: I would forget it fain;
> But, O! it presses to my memory,
> Like damned guilty deeds to sinners' minds:
> "Tybalt is dead, and Romeo banished";
> That—"banished", that one word "banished",
> Hath slain ten thousand Tybalts. Tybalt's death
> Was woe enough, if it had ended there:
> Or,—if sour woe delights in fellowship,
> And needly will be rank'd with other griefs,
> Why follow'd not, when she said "Tybalt's dead,"
> Thy father, or thy mother, nay, or both,
> Which modern lamentation might have moved?
> But with a rearward following Tybalt's death,
> "Romeo is banished"—to speak that word,
> Is father, mother, Tybalt, Romeo, Juliet,

All slain, all dead. "Romeo is banished"—
There is no end, no limit, measure, bound,
In that word's death; no words can that woe sound.

From *Romeo and Juliet*, SHAKESPEARE.

Hamlet.

To be, or not to be—that is the question—
Whether 'tis nobler in the mind to suffer
The slings and arrows of outrageous fortune,
Or to take arms against a sea of troubles,
And by opposing end them? To die—to sleep—
No more; and, by a sleep, to say we end
The heartache, and the thousand natural shocks
That flesh is heir to—'tis a consummation
Devoutly to be wish'd. To die—to sleep—
To sleep: perchance to dream—ay, there's the rub;
For in that sleep of death what dreams may come,
When we have shuffled off this mortal coil,
Must give us pause: there's the respect
That makes calamity of so long life;
For who would bear the whips and scorns of time,
The oppressor's wrong, the proud man's contumely,
The pangs of despised love, the laws delay,
The insolence of office, and the spurns
That patient merit of the unworthy takes,
When he himself might his quietus make
With a bare bodkin? who would fardels bear,
To grunt and sweat under a weary life,
But that the dread of something after death—
The undiscover'd country, from whose bourn
No traveller returns—puzzles the will,
And makes us rather bear those ills we have,
Than fly to others that we know not of?
Thus conscience does make cowards of us all,
And thus the native hue of resolution
Is sicklied o'er with the pale cast of thought,
And enterprises of great pith and moment,
With this regard, their currents turn awry
And lose the name of action.

From *Hamlet*, SHAKESPEARE.

There is also the vocal element of dramatic blank verse in which action dominates, but which will not be effective unless the dramatic intensity is projected through voice as well as through posture, gesture and deportment. Excerpts such as the following are recommended.

Volumnia.

        Nay, go not from us thus.
If it were so, that our request did tend
To save the Romans, thereby to destroy
The Volsces whom you serve, you might condemn us,
As poisonous of your honour: no; our suit
Is, that you reconcile them: while the Volsces
May say "This mercy we have shew'd": the Romans,
"This we received"; and each in either side
Give the all-hail to thee, and cry, "Be blest
For making up this peace!"   Thou know'st, great son,
The end of war's uncertain; but this certain,
That, if thou conquer Rome, the benefit
Which thou shalt thereby reap is such a name
Whose repetition will be dogg'd with curses;
Whose chronicle thus writ: "The man was noble,
But with his last attempt he wiped it out;
Destroy'd his country; and his name remains
To the ensuing age abhorr'd."   Speak to me, son:
Thou hast affected the fine strains of honour,
To imitate the graces of the gods;
To tear with thunder the wide cheeks o' the air,
And yet to charge thy sulphur with a bolt
That should but rive an oak.   Why dost not speak?
Think'st thou it honourable for a noble man
Still to remember wrongs?—Daughter, speak you:
He cares not for your weeping.—Speak thou, boy:
Perhaps thy childishness will move him more
Than can our reasons.—There's no man in the world
More bound to his mother, yet here he lets me prate
Like one i' the stocks.   Thou hast never in thy life
Shew'd thy dear mother any courtesy;

When she, poor hen, fond of no second brood,
Has cluck'd thee to the wars, and safely home,
Loaden with honour.   Say my request's unjust,
And spurn me back: but if it be not so,
Thou art not honest; and the gods will plague thee,
That thou restrain'st from me the duty which
To a mother's part belongs—He turns away:
Down, ladies; let us shame him with our knees.
To his surname Coriolanus 'longs more pride
Than pity to our prayers.   Down; an end:
This is the last:—so we will home to Rome,
And die among our neighbours.—Nay, behold us:
This boy, that cannot tell what he would have,
But kneels and holds up hands for fellowship,
Does reason our petition with more strength
Than thou hast to deny't.—Come, let us go:
This fellow had a Volscian to his mother;
His wife is in Corioli, and his child
Like him by chance.—Yet give us our despatch:
I am hush'd until our city be afire,
And then I'll speak a little.

From *Coriolanus*, SHAKESPEARE.

Queen Katherine.

Sir, I desire you do me right and justice,
And to bestow your pity on me; for
I am a most poor woman, and a stranger,
Born out of your dominions; having here
No judge indifferent, nor no more assurance
Of equal friendship and proceeding. Alas, sir,
In what have I offended you? what cause
Hath my behaviour given to your displeasure,
That thus you should proceed to put me off,
And take your good grace from me?   Heaven witness,
I have been to you a true and humble wife,
At all times to your will conformable;
Ever in fear to kindle your dislike,
Yea, subject to your countenance—glad or sorry,

As I saw it inclined.   When was the hour
I ever contradicted your desire,
Or made it not mine too?   Or which of your friends
Have I not strove to love, although I knew
He were mine enemy? what friend of mine
That had to him derived your anger, did I
Continue in my liking? nay, gave notice
He was from thence discharged?   Sir, call to mind
That I have been your wife, in this obedience,
Upward of twenty years, and have been blest
With many children by you: if, in the course
And process of this time you can report,
And prove it too, against mine honour aught,
My bond to wedlock, or my love and duty,
Against your sacred person, in God's name,
Turn me away; and let the foul'st contempt
Shut door upon me, and so give me up
To the sharp'st kind of justice.   Please you, sir,
The king, your father, was reputed for
A prince most prudent, of an excellent
And unmatch'd wit and judgment: Ferdinand,
My father, king of Spain, was reckon'd one
The wisest prince that there had reign'd by many
A year before: it is not to be question'd
That they had gather'd a wise council to them
Of every realm, that did debate this business,
Who deem'd our marriage lawful: wherefore I humbly
Beseech you, Sir, to spare me, till I may
Be by my friends in Spain advised; whose counsel
I will implore: if not, i' the name of God,
Your pleasure be fulfill'd!

From *Henry VIII*, SHAKESPEARE.

Duke of Buckingham.

　　　　　All good people,
You that thus far have come to pity me,
Hear what I say, and then go home and lose me.

I have this day received a traitor's judgment,
And by that name must die: yet, heaven bear witness,
And if I have a conscience, let it sink me,
Even as the axe falls, if I be not faithful!
The law I bear no malice for my death;
It has done, upon the premises, but justice:
But those that sought it I could wish more Christians:
Be what they will, I heartily forgive them:
Yet let them look they glory not in mischief,
Nor build their evils on the graves of great men;
For then my guiltless blood must cry against 'em.
For further life in this world I ne'er hope,
Nor will I sue, although the king have mercies
More than I dare make faults.   You few that loved me,
And dare be bold to weep for Buckingham,
His noble friends and fellows, whom to leave
Is only bitter to him, only dying,
Go with me, like good angels, to my end;
And, as the long divorce of steel falls on me,
Make of your prayers one sweet sacrifice,
And lift my soul to heaven.

From Henry VIII, SHAKESPEARE.

Mark Antony.

O, pardon me, thou bleeding piece of earth,
That I am meek and gentle with these butchers!
Thou art the ruins of the noblest man
That ever livèd in the tide of times.
Woe to the hand that shed this costly blood!
Over thy wounds now do I prophesy—
Which, like dumb mouths, do ope their ruby lips,
To beg the voice and utterance of my tongue—
A curse shall light upon the limbs of men;
Domestic fury and fierce civil strife
Shall cumber all the parts of Italy;

Blood and destruction shall be so in use,
And dreadful objects so familiar,
That mothers shall but smile when they behold
Their infants quarter'd with the hands of war;
All pity choked with custom of fell deeds:
And Cæsar's spirit ranging for revenge,
With Até by his side, come hot from hell,
Shall in these confines, with a monarch's voice,
Cry "Havoc!" and let slip the dogs of war;
That this foul deed shall smell above the earth
With carrion men, groaning for burial.

From *Julius Cæsar*, SHAKESPEARE.

There are some general observations to be made which affect the attitude of the speaker and which govern the presentation of all selections.

ATMOSPHERE is of supreme importance. It begins with a knowledge of the context, and a full understanding of the sense of the excerpt under consideration, followed by a sensitive perception of the mood, and it is established by intense concentration, both emotionally and intellectually. This mental concentration is applied before a selection is begun and it is not released until after the selection is finished. Atmosphere depends almost entirely upon this non-material concentration, and no amount of visual effect, by the aid of costume, props, stage settings and other devices, can compensate for its absence. A performance may even be technically weak and set in unimpressive surroundings, but it can have atmosphere through mental concentration and projection. Moreover, the concentration must not fluctuate; it must increase in strength as the performance progresses in order to develop strong climax.

If the mental effort just suggested is applied, it will affect the speech, and will provide the right stimulus for vocal intensity which is of much more use than the more obvious possibility of increased volume which is of least importance in connection with climax. Physical intensity of speech is the result of firm articulation, giving crispness and definition to the enunciation, it assists audibility and at the same time supplies vocal indication of mental concentration. Thus projection is both physical and mental, but the mental is certainly not least in importance.

Lastly, poor technique is usually obtrusive: the better the technique, the less noticeable it will be, provided the speaker is prepared to develop a reposeful manner, to aim at simplicity of style, and to adopt an attitude of complete sincerity in his presentations.

EXERCISES consist of revising all selections in this and in the previous chapter; applying, as considered appropriate, the technique which has now been adequately surveyed. The following summarised advice is offered, and the student should glance at the suggestions frequently until he finds himself applying them unconsciously.

1. Read the exercise silently.

2. If it is an excerpt, make certain of the context from which it is taken.

3. Ascertain the meaning of all words and phrases about which there is any doubt or obscurity.

4. Note the author, and consider the character involved, if any, and the dominant emotion or emotions.

5. "Feel" yourself into the mood—and character (if the selection is a dramatic excerpt).

6. Make sure that you have a physical basis of repose.

7. Concentrate mentally before beginning the selection.

8. Apply technique to develop climax, but remember that climax is just as much dependent upon increased mental concentration.

9. Projection must never become entirely physical; mental projection is much more important.

10. Prolong concentration until after concluding.

The final advice just given may look formidable, but it is reasonable; and by its application the student can become expressive in speech and adept in putting into practice the principles which underlie sound interpretation and convincingness of rendering. The student can be assured that the end is worthy of the means.

CHAPTER 6

BREATHING

Having laid the foundations of clear and expressive speech, it is necessary to give some attention to voice production. By a study of breathing, resonance, and voice placing, it should be possible to develop adequate audibility, without destroying the clarity or the expressiveness of speech. Many untrained speakers rely too much upon vocal quantity, not realising that too much voice will drown a loose articulation, while clear speech will be coherently received even when supported by only a small voice. The right balance is important. Clear enunciation is a primary necessity; that this shall easily be heard, and that it shall be attractive to listen to, it should be projected by a voice that is sufficient in quantity and pleasing in tonal quality. If there is any doubt about speech formation or expression, the previous chapters should be revised and the exercises repeated before proceeding further. If the student is confident about his speech, then he should continue by a careful consideration of breathing in the light of its being the motive power of voice.

It is impossible to overestimate the importance of breathing in connection with speech training. Effective voice production depends almost entirely upon an adequate supply of breath, judiciously controlled. Intensive anatomical study is quite unessential, but it is nevertheless impracticable to discuss the question of correct breathing without a working knowledge of the respiratory system. With the help of the diagram (Fig. 3), the following physical facts, with reference to the shape of the lungs and the relative strength and position of the

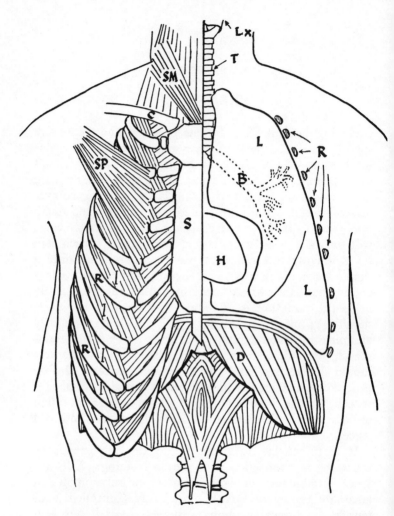

FIG. 3.—General arrangement of organs used in breathing. Half of the sternum and part of the ribs have been cut away to expose the left lung. Lx, larynx. T, trachea. B, bronchus. L, lung. H, heart. R, ribs. C, clavicle. SP, small pectoral muscle. SM, sterno-mastoid muscle. S, sternum. I, intercostal muscles. D, diaphragm.

controlling muscles, should enable the student to understand why the "Intercostal-diaphragmatic" method of breathing, controlled by the "Abdominal press", is generally advocated for purposes of voice production.

The lungs occupy almost the whole of the thorax. They are conical in shape, are composed mainly of minute air sacs, and, except where attached to the bronchi and where the blood vessels connect them with the heart, they are normally free. The lungs are covered with a delicate serous membrane known as the pleura, and they are effectively protected by the bony framework of the chest. The ribs, of which there are twelve pairs, form a series of curved bones all of which are posteriorly articulate with the spinal column. Anteriorly, the upper seven ribs join the sternum (breast-bone); the cartilages of the next three are each connected to the cartilage of the rib immediately above and are, therefore, called false ribs; while the extremities of the lowest two ribs are entirely free and are known as floating ribs. Intercostal muscles occupy the spaces between the ribs, and the ribs are connected to both spine and shoulders by the top rib muscles. The diaphragm is a powerful muscle, separating the abdomen from the thorax, and is co-ordinated with the abdominal muscles which lie over the stomach and under the spread of the ribs from the sternum. Fig. 3 should make this simple description clear, and as far as possible the various parts mentioned should be identified and located in the student's own body.

In order to breathe in, the thorax is increased in size by muscular action, and lungs are drawn outwards and downwards as the chest-wall expands and the diaphragm flattens, in consequence of which air is sucked in through the nose, pharynx, larynx, trachea and the bronchi, and finally reaches the lungs. As the chest is allowed to return to its lesser capacity the air is exhaled. Physiologically, the function of the lungs is to absorb and retain

I

oxygen from the air and to eject the undesirable carbon dioxide. In speech activity, however, the lungs are regarded as the means of supplying the breath in order to energise the vocal cords into the initial vibration from which vocal tone is developed.

The complete process of respiration embraces two sets of actions: those causing inspiration, upon the efficacy of which depends the adequacy of the breath supply; and those responsible for expiration, supremely important in voice production, because the quality and power of utterance are dependent upon the prudent management of the outgoing breath stream.

Intercostal-diaphragmatic breathing, as its name implies, relies mainly upon the action of the intercostal muscles, the diaphragm and the abdominal muscles, and it is undoubtedly the most effective method of breathing, for adequacy and for control. During inspiration, the top rib muscles raise the two upper ribs, and each external intercostal muscle draws upwards (and necessarily outwards) the rib immediately below; while the diaphragm, being well flattened, spreads all round, its action being comparable to that of a suction pump. For simple expiration, the process is more or less reversed. The air is exhaled through the compression of the lungs by the rebound of ribs and the rise of the diaphragm, due to relaxation of the muscles concerned. This is the breathing necessitated by normal exertion, and forms the basis, but only the basis, of breathing for voice production which must now be discussed in greater detail.

The actions associated with breathing-in for voice production are, to all intents and purposes, as described in the previous paragraph, but for the sake of clarity they might well be enumerated as follows:

1. The upper chest is expanded forwards, by the contraction of the small pectoral muscles.

2. The ribs swing outwards and upwards. This movement begins with the top ribs, and the movement is transmitted downwards by the intercostal muscles.

3. The diaphragm, by its own contraction, flattens and causes an all-round expansion of the body at about the level of the lowest five ribs.

4. The abdominal muscles are sufficiently relaxed to relieve any undue pressure on the digestive organs which lie beneath the diaphragm.

The external indications of the actions mentioned above are indicated with intentional exaggeration in Fig. 4.

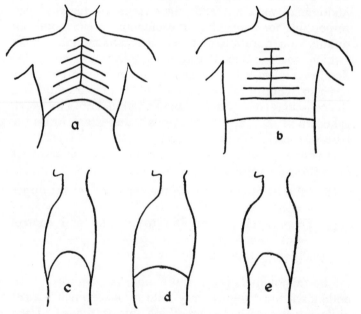

FIG. 4.—Exaggerated effects of movements for breathing. (a) and (b) chest capacity reduced and increased by movements of ribs and diaphragm. Side views: (c) before inspiration, (d) full inspiration, (e) expiration for voice production. Note: no collapse of the upper chest

Breathing-out for voice is necessarily a controlled expiration. It must never become a collapse of the thoracic cage due to uncontrolled rebound of the elastic framework, such as happens in ordinary normal breathing as muscular tension is released. During ordinary breathing the inspiration takes longer than the expiration; for controlled breathing the expiration must be economised to its longest possible duration, whilst inspiration has frequently to be adequately performed during a momentary pause.

It is desirable that the upper chest shall not collapse during speech. The diaphragm is co-ordinated with the abdominal muscles, and these muscles together are responsible for controlling the outgoing breath, both for quality and duration of tone. The abdominal muscles (which were relaxed during inspiration, while the diaphragm became contracted) are now contracted in order to "control the relaxation" of the diaphragm. It is the conscious contraction of the abdominal muscles which is known as the "abdominal press", and which forms the basis of conscious breath control.

It is now possible to enumerate the muscular activities of controlled expiration.

(1) Muscles associated with the expansion of the upper chest remain contracted.
(2) Diaphragm relaxes, but to prolong and control this process, the co-ordinated
(3) abdominal muscles are contracted.

The abdominal press must not be confused with abdominal breathing, a very mild form of which is used quite unconsciously for breathing during repose. Used consciously, abdominal breathing is physically harmful and is certainly inadequate by itself to support vocal effort.

While on the subject of harmful habits in breathing, the student should note the importance of avoiding any tendency towards clavicular breathing, an extremely dangerous respiratory habit in which the clavicle (collar bone) and the top ribs only are used, and merely the upper part of the chest inflated. It is, of course, inadequate for normal exertion, and it is not only physically dangerous, but causes rigidity of the throat and results immediately in impoverished tone. Clavicular breathing is nature's way of increasing the respiratory power during extreme exertion. Occasionally, the movements associated with this form of breathing are simulated to give certain emotional and dramatic effects. In actual practice, if the student concentrates on the region of the diaphragm, clavicular breathing will be almost impossible.

As a means of maintaining the organs of speech in a healthy condition there is ample reason to repeat that, except during actual vocalisation, air should enter through the nose, the function of which is to purify, moisten and warm the air before it reaches the throat and lungs. If the presence of any obstruction to the normal passage of air through the nose is detected, it should be attended to without delay. The technique of nasal surgery has, during the last few years, so greatly improved that it is unnecessarily foolish to attempt vocal development of any kind (to say nothing of jeopardising the general health) while adenoids, deviated septum, or any other form of obstruction is present.

In concluding this chapter, the following points are repeated for the sake of emphasis. Breathing, although a means to an end, must be adequate and controlled if speech training is to develop satisfactorily. Clavicular and abdominal methods must be avoided, and an all-round expansion developed at the level of the diaphragm. Control is best accomplished by the diaphragm being assisted by the abdominal muscles, this combined action giving, during expiration, a consciousness of definite abdominal pressure. During inhalation, breath should be taken in through the nose, but during speech it is generally necessary to breath through the nose and mouth. The whole purpose of breathing exercises is to lessen the time taken for complete inspiration, and to develop control over the prolonged expiration.

EXERCISES for breathing must begin with—

1. Exercises for FLEXIBILITY. Vigorously shake, (i) the hands from the wrists, (ii) the forearms from the elbow, (iii) the arms from the shoulders, (iv) each foot from the ankle, and (v) each leg from the knee, until there is a consciousness of complete freedom from muscular rigidity.

2. RELAXATION. More will be said about relaxation in the appropriate chapter yet to come. For the present it must be pointed out that (a) all physical conditions should be the result of mental feeling, (b) relaxation is best achieved as a "rebound" from "stretching", and (c) relaxation can be most easily encouraged by free rhythmic movements made to the rhythmic sounds of appropriate music.

(i) In a recumbent position, or standing with easy posture (the former if convenient), stretch the upper part of the body away from the lower "until it hurts" —that is, until a feeling of discomfort is felt—then relax on the natural rebound. Feel the stretch pass from the toes up to the top of the head. (ii) Repeat similarly with the arms, extending the finger-tips downwards, feeling the stretch pass from them up to the shoulders. (iii) With arms raised, and standing on the toes, stretch upwards, then relax on the rebound.

> *N.B.*—Remember, it is the rebound to relaxation which is important; the stretch is merely a useful means of approach by contrast.

3. POSTURE. (i) Roll the head around on the neck, and find the place where "it balances itself" with the least muscular strain. (ii) "Roll" the shoulders (with arms hanging loosely downwards) in a rotation, upwards in front and downwards at the back. Allow them finally to settle, easily held back without stiffness, and held downwards by the weight of the loosely hanging arms. (iii) Lift the upper part of the body (from the waist upwards) away from the lower part—"out of the pelvis" as it were. This will be quite simple if approached by the right mental attitude, imagining that the upper part of the body is "buoyant". (iv) With the knees held back, but not "braced", and the feet somewhat apart, feel the weight of the symmetrical body swaying lightly on the balls of the feet, steadied only by the heels lightly touching the ground: sway gently forwards and backwards, and also in a rotating motion, and finally adopt that posture found by experiment to demand the least feeling of muscular effort. (v) Repeat the above frequently until the position becomes habitual, or certainly until it may be assumed quickly and easily.

4. CAPACITY. Breathe in and out to your own "natural" rhythm, concentrating mentally and encouraging physically the maximum activity in the region of the diaphragm by holding the tips of the fingers lightly against the spread of the ribs, or alternatively on the same horizontal level but in the centre (about two or three inches below the lower end of the sternum, and vertically below it). Make sure your wrists, arms and shoulders are relaxed, and while observing the outward movements, keep in your mind the internal actions described previously in this chapter.

5. BREATH CONTROL. (i) Place the hands, with palms lightly against the chest and in a horizontal position, so that the balls of the thumbs are resting on the spread of the floating ribs and the finger-tips meeting over the space between them. (ii) Breathe in, feeling both a sideways expansion and a frontal expansion of ribs and of diaphragm respectively. Do not attempt ever to "hold the breath" (which always tends to cause rigidity), but when the movements seem to have reached their maximum position without strain, (iii) breathe out, preferably counting aloud, 1, 2, 3, etc., at a rate of about one second for each number, while drawing in the muscles under the finger-tips and trying to avoid a collapse of the ribs under the palms of the hands. Make sure to revise the description of the abdominal press before performing this exercise. The gradual increase of the maximum number reached in counting will give some indication of progress.

General comments in connection with the above exercises must be made to ensure the right order and attitude. The exercises in breathing should be conscientiously carried out before the student proceeds to attempt tonal development. They should be performed intelligently; the student should know why the various movements are recommended. Whenever possible, the exercises should be accompanied by appropriate music. The nose must be free from obstruction; it is not only children who need to be reminded of handkerchief drill prior to breathing exercises.

The order in which the exercises are performed is of vital importance, and the following is suggested for practical purposes with the normal class or student. Exercises for (a) Flexibility, (b) Relaxation, (c) Posture, (d) Capacity, (e) Control, and then, (f) relaxation, (g)

capacity, (*h*) control, repeating (*f*), (*g*) and (*h*), checking and correcting posture, and repeating exercises for
flexibility as required.

The student is advised to work on breathing exercises
"little and often". Strain, as the result of over-prolonged
exercising, leads to boredom and rigidity, and results
in harmful physical habits and unintelligent mental
control.

CHAPTER 7

VOICE PRODUCTION

One of the simplest ways of understanding how the human voice is produced is by analogy, considering its mechanism side by side with that of the pneumatic type of motor-horn. The following comparisons should be studied in connection with Fig. 5.

The working of the motor-horn is simple enough to follow. Air is expelled from the rubber bulb when gripped by the motor-driver. At the junction of the bulb and horn is a reed which is free to vibrate in the stream of air ejected from the bulb. This vibration, a small buzzing sound, is reinforced in, and projected by, the horn as a kind of musical sound of considerable volume. The reed is designed to function in an air stream of only one direction and thus remains inactive while air is sucked into the bulb in readiness for the next blast when required. We have, therefore, several clearly defined factors, namely, (1) muscular effort, controlling (2) a supply of air which sets into vibration (3) a reed producing a sound which is developed acoustically in (4) a resonating horn.

It should be clearly understood that none of these factors is indispensable. If the student can obtain an old-fashioned motor-horn, it would be worth while his making the following simple experiments. After one or two "normal" blasts with steady bulb pressure, (a) try compressing the bulb very slowly. It will be found possible to deflate the bulb completely but at so slow a rate that the reed is not set into vibration. (b) Compress the bulb violently. Vigorous, uncontrolled compression will probably have the effect of producing anything but a

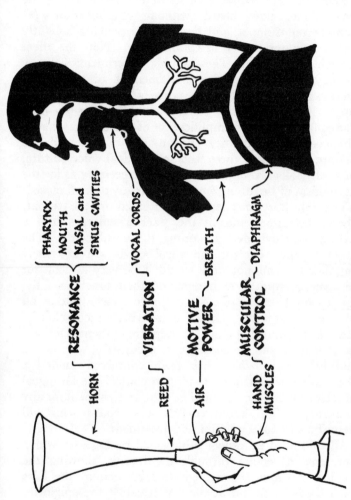

FIG. 5.—The voice compared, by analogy, with a motor horn

pleasant sound. (*c*) Remove the "trumpet" and observe the comparative weakness of the sound produced by the reed alone, now heard without amplification. (*d*) Replace the trumpet, and muffle it by packing it lightly with soft material such as cotton-waste. Note the effect of such obstruction. These simple experiments will, by analogy, demonstrate the fundamentals of voice production as being (1) the importance of a controlled breath supply, (2) the necessity of laryngeal vibration (by itself inadequate), and (3) amplification of voice by resonance which develops quantity and quality of tone. Before attempting to apply these facts in practical voice culture, some physiological descriptions are as necessary as for the mechanism of breathing which has already been discussed.

The vibratory mechanism is situated in the throat, where the upper end of the trachea enlarges into a cartilaginous cylinder containing the vocal cords. The muscles which control the vocal cords are extremely complicated, and not only would it be very difficult for the average student to understand their functions fully, but it would be dangerous for him to concentrate at all upon their activity. They function best unconsciously, and they control pitch by adjusting themselves instantaneously and, in most cases, accurately, to produce audibly a note which has been conceived mentally. The student should not attempt to control the laryngeal muscles consciously. Should he require treatment for any abnormality, he should consult a specialist who will prescribe without explaining his treatment.

All that need be known is indicated by Fig. (6), which represents a section through the larynx, showing the vocal cords, and above them (for protection) the false vocal cords. The lid at the top is called the epiglottis. The function of the vocal cords is to initiate vibration at the required pitch. The epiglottis, raised during breathing, is lowered during the act of swallowing food. Should any food, or foreign body of any sort, find its way past the epiglottis, it will, on coming into contact with the highly nerve-sensitive false vocal cords, be ejected by violent coughing, before it can reach the (true) vocal cords. The chink between the vocal cords, known as the glottis, is fully open for free inspiration, and becomes a rather

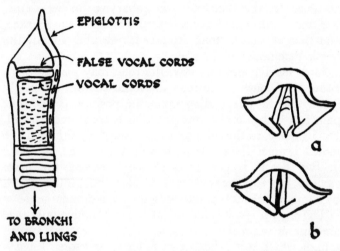

Fig. 6.—Side view sketch of larynx, simplified. Part of side wall removed to show vocal cords, false vocal cords and epiglottis

Fig. 7.—Freehand sketches showing positions of vocal cords for (a) inspiration, and (b) voice

narrow slit as the vocal cords adjust themselves to produce a sound, as shown in Fig. 7.

Among the resonators which influence the quality of tone are, firstly, the cavities of the larynx itself, affecting the vibration at, or close to, its source. It is doubtful whether these resonators are consciously or directly controllable. They must be accepted as given by nature, and should receive hygienic treatment in common with the rest of the vocal organs.

The next resonator above the larynx is the pharynx, over which the speaker has some control. The pharynx is constricted by muscles during the swallowing of food, and the act of swallowing may be consciously performed without any food being present. Of especial importance, however, is the fact that the pharynx, in its shape, size and condition, changes with the mood of the speaker, and thus affects the tone produced, reflecting vocally the speaker's emotional changes.

After leaving the pharynx, the tone may pass through either the mouth or through the nasal cavities (or partly through both), depending upon the position of the soft, palate, which can be brought under conscious control. For instance, in the final sound of "sing" ŋ, although the mouth is open, the sound is entirely a nasal one, as shown in Fig. 8. It is permitted to pass through the nasal cavities, but is prevented from passing through the mouth by contact of the soft palate with the back of the tongue.

The mouth is a resonator but it can produce only that amount of resonance associated with the various speech sounds which it is called upon to form, and some English speech sounds have extremely poor resonance, the aspirates having, of course, none at all. The worst possible mistake a speaker (or singer) can make is to distort any speech sound in an effort to improve its resonance. This fault causes badly trained singers to pronounce "love" as laːv or lɔːv, "hit" as hiːt, or hat as haːt or het.

In regard to mouth resonance, the speaker should make the most of each sound, especially the vowels. He should keep his mouth as widely open through a loosely dropped jaw, and his lips as rounded and as protruded, only as far as is consistent with accurate pronunciation. So far as he can, without changing the vowel's characteristic quality, he should avoid a throaty tone, keeping the tongue from unnecessarily bunching up at the back of the mouth by keeping the tip of the tongue in light contact with the back surfaces of the lower front teeth. The mouth and its organs are used to enunciate clear speech, not to produce loud voice. Resonance should be

Fig. 8.—Diagram of contact for ŋ sound

developed in the pharynx, in the nasal cavities, and in the sinuses of the head.

The pharynx is the first resonator to receive the vibrating air-stream as it leaves the larynx. As has already been stated, pharyngeal resonance is affected by the emotional condition of the speaker. Nervous tension causes rigidity of the constrictor muscles and results in restricted tone. Conversely, a sense of repose will allow relaxation of the pharyngeal constrictors, and a full tone of warm quality can be developed. The application of these physical facts is obvious and will add further proof to the advice that a calm mind and a reposeful body are of primary importance in all activities of speech and voice.

There are various ways in which pharyngeal resonance may be consciously developed and controlled. "Open throat production" is a term widely used professionally, the technique of which is not only concerned with tone production but also with attack and control, and the student will find it especially profitable to consider this matter very carefully.

It is possible to control breath by laryngeal constriction, and indeed many specialists used to advocate this as a sound method of attack. It has, however, for some time been held to be extremely dangerous and it is doubtful if any specialists continue to advocate the *Coup de Glotte* as it was called, although it is still to be heard when untrained speakers and singers attack initial vowels with what can only be described as a very slight coughing sound in the throat. Such performers, failing to control their breathing from the diaphragm, compress the breath in the larynx, and then release it by suddenly removing the obstruction, the vocal cords adjusting themselves instantaneously to give the desired pitch. Conscious attention to correct breath control will do much to "overcome (this) evil with good", but there are more direct methods which should be tried by all students not only as correction from any tendency to glottal breath control, but as a positive approach to good tone.

One such approach is based on a mental awareness of a simple acoustic fact—that sound is transmitted through air as a medium, and that if the medium is continuous and is not obstructed, then the communication will be more efficient. An acceptance of this fact and the mental conception of a pulsating air-stream continuous from the diaphragm of the speaker to the ear-drum of the farthest member of his audience, has a psychological effect which, by suggestion, tends to open the narrower parts of the respiratory tract. It is simple enough; the physical fundamentals are sound, and, in regard to voice, most speakers are very auto-suggestible. Merely by thinking this out, and by immediate experiment, the tone of many speakers becomes much improved.

Another approach is based upon the physiological behaviour of the throat during inspiration and expiration, and a simple experiment is suggested. Inhale a deep breath with the mouth wide open—take it in as if it were the first gasp of sea air after spending many months in a hot, dusty city. Then, breathe out, singing any vowel. When breathing-in, the throat is almost bound to feel more "open" than when exhaling on a sound, and this sensation is physiologically justified. A number of speakers and singers "close" the throat unnecessarily for voice production, and it is suggested that this fault can be prevented by imagining that breath is being drawn in while actually it is, of course, being expelled on a vocal tone. This idea forms the basis of a method successfully employed by a number of voice-training specialists whose method is to encourage the pupil to imagine that his voice is at the far end of the studio before he starts to sing, and that he is drawing it into himself instead of projecting it out. This suggestion has the psychological effect of the pupil concentrating on breathing in, while singing out, and the reflex actions of the muscles cause the throat to attempt to adjust itself for the more widely open positions of inspiration.

Other methods include attacking a vowel preceded by an aspirate, and reducing the "h" sound so that it is no longer noticeable as a breath sound, but attempting to keep the sensation of its being pronounced in order to keep the throat open.

Mention should be made of one last method of acquiring

K

an open throat and pharynx. Most students will be able to induce themselves into yawning, and by experiment will find that during a yawn it is not only possible to experience real intercostal-diaphragmatic breathing at its fullest, but also to experience a complete freedom of the entire vocal mechanism. By shaping a vocalised yawn into a vowel sound, it is possible to develop a warmth and fulness of tone hardly attainable by other means.

The student should experiment with all the approaches mentioned, and having found out which of them seem to promise the best results to him individually, he should, either by his own resourcefulness or under the guidance of his tutor, adapt them for use in revised practice of vowels, leading to improved tone in continuous speech.

After passing through the pharynx, the voice has the alternative possibilities of passing through the mouth to vocalise speech, or of passing through the nasal cavities from which it can acquire still greater resonance. Nasal resonance must not be confused with that unpleasant timbre referred to, erroneously, as a nasal tone. So-called nasal tone is in reality a tone produced without nasal resonance. In producing brilliancy of tone, the nasal cavities, and the various sinus cavities which communicate with them, are the main sources of the overtones and harmonics which are characteristic of voices usually described as "interesting" and "attractive".

In developing nasal resonance, there are several clearly marked stages, the first of which is the forming of healthy respiratory habits and, therefrom, a wholesome condition of the nasal cavities. Hygienic habits, including the frequent use of a handkerchief, habitual nose-breathing, the avoidance of places where the contents of the atmosphere are likely to irritate the mucous surfaces of the nose, all these are matters about which a sensible attitude may surely be taken for granted.

The next stage is the development, by exercise, of a

healthy muscular tone in the soft palate as the controlling valve of nasal resonance. Most difficulties with regard to nasal resonance are caused by the soft palate muscles having become atrophied by lack of use. Nasal resonance frequently begins to produce itself immediately the soft palate is brought under conscious control. For this purpose use is made of the various consonants which depend on activity of the soft palate, such as g, k, and ŋ.

The final stage is rather more difficult to describe than to demonstrate, and it will best be understood if approached experimentally. The student should not concern himself with physical explanations; he should rely upon psychological suggestion and upon aural perception of tone quality.

(1) Hum a continuous ŋ sound (not an "m" hum, which is rather more difficult for this purpose).

(2) While continuing the hum through the nose, make the articulatory movements of "My mother minds my money", but without allowing any voice to pass through the mouth.

(3) Practise well stage (2) (above) until it can be easily performed with (a) all the voice passing through the nose, and (b) with the articulatory movements firm enough to be "lip-read".

(4) Begin a repetition of (2) (above), but during the exercise allow some voice gradually to pass out through the mouth so that speech becomes vocalised whilst tone is still associated with the nasal cavities.

(5) Repeat (4) (above) until a balance is achieved between (a) passing through the mouth the minimum quantity of voice for speech sounds (which rely mostly upon firm articulation), and (b) consciously allowing the greater part of the voice, not required for speech formation, to remain associated with nasal resonance.

One last word about soft palate activity. When breathing through the nose, the soft palate is normally relaxed and hangs limply downwards. For spontaneous vocal attack, the soft palate needs to be in a state of tonicity and this is achieved by breathing through nose and mouth during continuous speech activity. Breathing through nose and mouth is, in fact, necessary for reasons of adequacy of breathing and also in connection with the open throat previously advocated.

The student is bound, sooner or later, to hear the expression "voice placing". He should not interpret the term literally; it is used by way of psychological suggestion. Assuming the physical requirements of good tone are present, the achievement of "forward tone" depends finally upon mental control. In other words, given a sound physical basis, the voice will go where it is willed to go by the speaker.

To put this matter more clearly, and in correct sequence, the physical essentials are: adequate breathing controlled by the abdominal press; an "open" throat; a feeling of freedom and relaxation of all the muscles, especially those associated with shoulders, neck and jaw; and a right resonantal balance between nasal, pharyngeal and oral resonances. These physical essentials are of no avail, however, unless the voice is mentally conceived as being forward in placing. The old-time actor, groping perhaps in unscientific darkness, had his methods, based upon practical experience, of "feeling the voice in the mask". The student must, likewise, "feel" the voice into the sinus cavities of the cheeks and the forehead.

Voice is not confined to the vocal organs; it will transmit itself wherever there is air as its medium. Voice is, in reality, more outside than inside the speaker, and it should be so conceived. It is also true that, other things being equal, a musical sound will carry more effectively than a transient noise. Regarded thus, voice becomes the "carrier wave" upon which speech is superimposed.

Finally, the student must not be bewildered by the most important advice that he should not rely upon beauty of tone. It may seem difficult for him to understand that fundamental tone quality, once developed, is rarely used in its most beautiful capacity. To use the voice expressively, it is necessary to discriminate between beauty of fundamental tone, and expressiveness by means of change of tone colour. The voice cannot become expressive without a good basic tone upon which to build a rendering, but it can be inexpressive if the same unchanged fundamental tone is used continuously. The worst performers are those who rely upon a beautiful voice which they use indiscriminately in all their programmes. The sensitive artist is never afraid to obscure his fundamental tone, however beautiful, to indicate mood and character which may not be beautiful.

EXERCISES necessitate frequent reference to the theory of voice production outlined in this chapter. The exercises must be approached intelligently and with the constant attention of conscious aural analysis.

(1) BREATHING. Precede all vocal exercises by several exercises in breathing, with special attention to relaxation and repose, without which no warmth or fulness of tone can ever be achieved.

(2) SOFT PALATE EXERCISES. Vocalise,

in̬ in̬ in̬ etc., ɔŋ ɔŋ ɔŋ etc.,

and similarly with other vowels.

Repeat continuously gɔŋgɔŋgɔŋgɔŋgɔŋ etc.

(3) NASAL RESONANCE. Humming on n, on m, and on ŋ. Keep the mouth open for the n and ŋ, but make sure that all the sound is passing through the nose.

(4) RESONANTAL BALANCE. Revise the appropriate parts of this chapter, and practise on

nuː nɔː nɑː neː niː
muː mɔː mɑː meː miː

(5) ATTACK. Revise the appropriate parts of this chapter, and practise on uː ɔː ɑː eː iː making sure that the throat and associated organs are free and "open", and that the impulse is from the diaphragm.

(6) RANGE OF PITCH AND FLEXIBILITY. Repeat the exercises from (2) to (5) (above) on all pitches within easy vocal range, descending and ascending by semitones. Repeat the same exercise on ascending and descending inflections, extended as far as possible within the range of the voice without straining.

(7) CO-ORDINATION. Choose some phrases either from or similar to the exercises in the chapter on vowels, and practise consciously on co-ordinating all the factors involved: relaxation, repose, breathing, attack, resonance, placing and projection.

(8) CHANGE OF TONE COLOUR. Revise the exercises for tone colour on pages 69–73.

CHAPTER 8

MOVEMENT

Movement is very definitely allied to speech. It is so important that this chapter might well have taken first place in the book had it not been assumed that the student would have made a first reading, cursorily, to view the entire field. This chapter might well be regarded as the beginning of a more careful review in which each factor may be studied in its right perspective to the whole subject.

Apart from a general acceptance of the necessity of physical education, there are a number of specific reasons why good movement is fundamental in speech training. These reasons should be noted by the student.

In connection with vocal development—

1. Good posture is essential in order that breathing may be both adequate and controlled.
2. Good tone depends upon good breathing and resonance, which are impossible unless there is complete freedom from muscular rigidity.

Firm articulation of speech is the result of precise muscular co-ordination, and it has been observed that—

3. Speakers with controlled muscular actions generally seem to show good response to speech training.

In regard to flexibility of rhythm in speech—

4. There is a close connection between rhythmic movement and rhythmic speech.

In its widest interpretation, speech training might well be defined as "Training in expressiveness", and—

5. In dramatic selections, characterisation is portrayed by body as well as by speech and voice.

For public work generally—

    6. Deportment is clearly connected with "presence", whether on a platform, in a class-room, on the stage, or in the committee room.

Lastly, the speaker who is tired stands little chance of projecting himself in speech, and—

    7. Fatigue of body, which prevents vitality of speech, may in many instances be prevented by habitual good posture and rhythmic everyday movements.

Any form of physical exercise should be preceded by RELAXATION and should lead to better reposefulness. It would not be wise to write at great length about relaxation. The ability to relax is developed from an attitude of mind, and only the student can decide which mental approach is best for him, which thoughts will radiate a sense of repose through his nervous system to the extremities of his body. Auto-suggestion plays an enormous part in acquiring the ability to relax at will, a habit which is now more than ever necessary to preserve mental serenity in spite of the strain of modern life. Whether it be from the philosopher, the psychologist, or the saint, from some such source the student should find the right mental approach, gaining that which will affect his whole life in relationships far outside the more specific scope of this subject.

With the right mental attitude, there are, however, physical methods of encouraging relaxation. For this purpose, the ideal position is to be found by lying flat in a comfortable attitude. If the support is unyielding, something should be placed under the neck and under the small of the back, to allow the spinal column to rest in its natural alignment. Stretching is the next step, arms and legs being stretched away from the shoulders and hips by mentally concentrating on pulling from fingers and toes respectively, at the same time stretching the head away from the shoulders. After this stretched position is held for as long as is comfortable, the release of concentration should result in a rebound to complete relaxation.

In the early stages it is necessary (and it is preferable at all times) that the body should feel as comfortable as possible; the environment should be quiet, and the room well-ventilated but not cold. Some find that absolute quietness helps while the mind is allowed to dwell upon a calm, peaceful scene; others find that suitable music assists in producing the right atmosphere.

Complete relaxation may be tested by the lifting up of the limbs by another person; when released they should fall with a thud. Complete relaxation should be practised as a matter of routine, and the term is used frequently to create the right feeling, but it is not strictly correct to use it in reference to actual performance. Absolute relaxation can result only in complete muscular collapse of the entire body. The justification of using the term is that it leads to the right mental conception of TONICITY.

Tonicity is the result of mental awareness and muscular preparedness—a state between complete relaxation and muscular contraction, but nearer to the former of these two extremes. An athlete at the "Get ready" stage is a good example of tonicity. Tonicity conserves energy because the readiness of response which it fosters means fewer false starts and more purposeful activity. Tonicity takes the strain from work; it prevents the writer from gripping his pen unnecessarily hard, and the driver his steering wheel. Tonicity prevents a sense of repose from becoming mere lifelessness.

Tonicity implies symmetry and balanced tension. The opposing forces necessary to achieve symmetry may be kept to their minimum provided they are equalised. This is important in the case of posture. A good posture, being symmetrical, relies upon balance and therefore requires little muscular effort to hold it. The slightest departure from symmetry immediately requires extra muscular control to attempt to stop more serious deviation which, however, occurs through muscular fatigue, and more effort than ever is then required to prevent complete collapse. This is the vicious circle which is the common cause of almost all faulty postures.

Good posture necessitates a consciousness of tonicity. It is as essential to avoid the common tendency of stiff rigidity (so frequently confused with good posture) as it is to avoid the slouching stance with its receding chest and protruding abdomen. To acquire good posture the abdominal muscles must again be referred to. Frequently the advice is given to the student that he should draw in the abdomen. It is much better to concentrate on "lifting" it (tucking the abdominal organs up under the domed diaphragm). There is a sensation of physical buoyancy which comes from the feeling that fully inflated lungs have the effect of lifting the weight of the upper part of the body from the lower part. It does not matter whether this is or is not physically true; it can be experienced by anyone with reasonable imagination.

A first approach to this matter has been suggested in the chapter on breathing. There are, of course, many other methods of approach, one of which is to lie down flat on the back, attempting to reproduce the lying posture when standing. It need hardly be said that no pillow is permitted in this method, the subject should lie flat on his back. In all methods the fundamental is the acquirement of that balanced poise which demands the least possible muscular effort.

Exercises in rhythmic movement are best performed in class under the direction of a qualified instructor, but the following notes on fundamentals might be useful. A sense of rhythm manifests itself in the activities of its possessor, and practice of any one rhythmic exercise will improve the general perception of rhythm and any or all of its more specific outlets. So that, apart from group work, the student can do much through such pursuits as music and dancing; and also in ordinary everyday activities, if he performs them to a tune, mentally (not necessarily orally) sung.

With a good sense of posture, and after some exercise in rhythmic movement, it should not be found difficult to acquire a smooth carriage. Provided the legs swing from the hips, and the mind dwells upon thoracic buoyancy and upon a tune of suitable rhythm, then there is no better device than the well-tried (and proved) method of walking with a book or similar object balanced on the head; the presence of such an object may be imagined for quite a long time after its removal.

The various methods of sitting, standing, and other conventional movements and positions fall outside the scope of this book, belonging strictly to the technique of dramatic art. One or two observations will, perhaps, be useful to the student who feels the urge to use gesture in rendering dramatic scenes. It should, however, be remembered at all times that gestures must be sparingly used on the platform. A gesture which may be quite convincing in a stage performance might appear most incongruous if used with the same abandon but without the many stage devices which would make it seem realistic. This advice must not be misunderstood; it certainly does not suggest the use of cramped gestures.

Exercises for flexibility should be practised regularly in order that gestures may be made convincingly when required. If the basic movements are habitually free, the gestures may be used in rehearsal and performance without specific practice.

In all movement, keep the diaphragm as the centre or hub about which all gestures and postures should be balanced. Arm movements, for example, although known to be mechanically radial from the wrist, the elbow, or the shoulder, should, nevertheless, be conceived as starting from the diaphragm and finishing at the finger-tips.

To give the effect of spontaneity to a rendering, the timing of gestures is of first importance. More perform-ances lack life through faulty timing than through any other cause, although timing is only the technical applica-tion of the natural co-ordination observed in everyday speech. The brain conceives a thought which is expressed first in the face, then by voice and by gesture if necessary. Technical timing is applied along the same lines. Whether the lines to be spoken have been learnt or are being read for the first time, there must be mental concentration upon them before speech begins. It is during this con-centration that atmosphere is created, greatly strengthened by facial responsiveness. Whether speech or gesture starts next depends upon the length of the phrase or sentence, for the two must be so synchronised as to allow the gesture to reach its final fillip simultaneously with the climactic word to be spoken. The release of a gesture will cause no trouble if there is flexibility of movement. The performer with stiff movements, having made a gesture, tends to become self-conscious about it, misses the right moment for its release and has to "place" his limbs, awkwardly and obviously, back into the right position, having, meanwhile, lost concentration on the meaning, and having destroyed any atmosphere he may have created.

A special point needs to be made about facial expressive-ness, if only because it is the one form of physical expression which should always be used, even if the performer is unseen, as for instance in broadcasting. Facial expression and tone colour are closely related. The smiling face causes muscular relaxation, which induces relaxation into the muscular systems of the face and neck generally. The muscles of the pharynx are especially responsive in this sense, and being relaxed will provide the tone associated with the smiling face. Conversely, a hard tone is extremely difficult, and for many performers impossible, to produce without a frowning face. Facial responsiveness usually follows mental concentration and a stimulated imagination. It is not restricted as gesture is restricted when clearly unsuitable for selections in which thought predominates. Appropriate facial responsiveness, so long as it indicates mental alertness, change of mood, and imaginative awareness, is inseparable from vocal expression, whether this be concerned with the most delicate lyric or the most boisterous farce.

In conclusion, there are certain fundamentals which need emphasising. Gesture must not be used to make up for lack of thought, neither must any form of movement be made without thought behind it. Movement, studied conscientiously and rehearsed constantly, is best used unconsciously during a performance. The deciding question is not "Can a gesture be used?" but rather "Is a gesture essential?" or better still: "Is it possible to do without gesture?" Even with vitality of thought, expressiveness of speech, and responsiveness of face, it is very easy to spoil a rendering by the use of one redundant gesture. Let movement support voice, and let gesture assist in characterisation or emphasis, but the spoken word must remain the most subtle and the most vital means of communication, the expressiveness of which must not be weakened by any inartistic physical distraction.

Exercises for Relaxation

(1) As suggested on page 134.
(2) Sitting on the floor, trunk upright and legs straight out, stretch out to touch the toes. Make the movement slowly and repeat to rhythm. Feel the stretch pass from the toes to the fingers. Relax to tonicity on the rebound after each repetition. Finally, relax completely recumbent.

EXERCISE FOR TONICITY

(1) Stretch as when waking from sleep, increasing the effort until a sense of strain is felt to be approaching.

(2) Completely relax, preferably by crumpling on to the floor.

(3) Stand symmetrically, but easily, and adopt tonicity by transmission to the body of mental control approaching either from (1) repeated, or by controlled relaxation from (2) repeated.

EXERCISES FOR THE ABDOMINAL MUSCLES

(1) (a) Lie flat (if necessary with feet under a low shelf) and raise the upper part of the body slowly to a sitting position.

(b) Return slowly to a lying position.

(c) Relax.

(2) (a) Lie flat on the back and raise both legs together.

(b) Perform the motions of pedal-cycling.

(c) Allow legs to return slowly to the floor.

(d) Relax.

EXERCISE FOR FLEXIBILITY, as prescribed on page 134, and also any free movements, preferably to rhythmic music.

EXERCISE FOR POSTURE

(1) Begin with exercise described on page 135.

(2) (a) Stand easily and with weight of the body taken by the balls of the feet.

(b) Raise the arms and hold them up until tiredness is experienced or imagined.

(c) Allow the arms to crumple and fall to the sides, swinging themselves before coming to rest.

EXERCISES FOR RHYTHMIC MOVEMENT. In addition to exercises specified by a class instructor, any form of dancing or movement to suitable music.

EXERCISE FOR DEPORTMENT

(a) Walk purposefully from corner to corner of a room, carrying a light object balanced on the head.

(b) Repeat at a leisurely pace.

(c) Repeat at increased speed.

This exercise should be performed to music in three appropriate tempos.

EXERCISES FOR TIMING OF GESTURES. Refer to selections illustrating Climax and Emphatic Stress (in the chapters on Vocal Expression and Interpretation and Rendering), timing appropriate gestures to synchronise with the climactic words.

SELECTIONS FOR STUDY AND PRACTICE

Now that I, tying thy glass mask tightly,
May gaze thro' these faint smokes curling whitely,
As thou pliest thy trade in this devil's-smithy—
Which is the poison to poison her, prithee?

He is with her; and they know that I know
Where they are, what they do: they believe my tears flow
While they laugh, laugh at me, at me fled to the drear
Empty church, to pray God in, for them!—I am here.

Grind away, moisten and mash up thy paste,
Pound at thy powder—I am not in haste!
Better sit thus, and observe thy strange things,
Than go where men wait me and dance at the King's.

That in the mortar—you call it a gum?
Ah, the brave tree whence such gold oozings come!
And yonder soft phial, the exquisite blue,
Sure to taste sweetly—is that poison too?

Had I but all of them, thee and thy treasures,
What a wild crowd of invisible pleasures!
To carry pure death in an earring, a casket,
A signet, a fan-mount, a fillagree-basket!

Soon, at the King's, a mere lozenge to give
And Pauline should have just thirty minutes to live!
And to light a pastile, and Elise, with her head,
And her breast, and her arms, and her hands, should drop
    dead!

Quick—is it finished?   The colour's too grim!
Why not soft like the phial's, enticing and dim?
Let it brighten her drink, let her turn it and stir,
And try it and taste, ere she fix and prefer!

What a drop!   She's not little, no minion like me—
That's why she ensnared him: this never will free
The soul from those strong, great eyes,—say, "no!"
To that pulse's magnificent come-and-go.

For only last night, as they whispered, I brought
My own eyes to bear on her so, that I thought
Could I keep them one half minute fixed, she would fall,
Shrivelled; she fell not; yet this does it all!

Not that I bid you spare her the pain!
Let death be felt and the proof remain;
Brand, burn up, bite into its grace—
He is sure to remember her dying face!

Is it done?   Take my mask off!   Nay, be not morose,
It kills her, and this prevents seeing it close:
The delicate droplet, my whole fortune's fee—
If it hurts her, beside, can it ever hurt me?

Now, take all my jewels, gorge gold to your fill,
You may kiss me, old man, on my mouth if you will!
But brush this dust off me, lest horror it brings
Ere I know it—next moment I dance at the King's!

The Laboratory, ROBERT BROWNING.

The sea is calm to-night.
The tide is full, the moon lies fair
Upon the Straits;—on the French coast the light
Gleams and is gone; the cliffs of England stand,
Glimmering and vast, out in the tranquil bay.

L

Come to the window, sweet is the night air!
Only, from the long line of spray
Where the sea meets the moon-blanch'd sand,
Listen! you hear the grating roar
Of pebbles which the waves draw back, and fling,
At their return, up the high strand,
Begin, and cease, and then again begin,
With tremulous cadence slow, and bring
The eternal note of sadness in.

Sophocles long ago
Heard it on the Ægean, and it brought
Into his mind the turbid ebb and flow
Of human misery; we
Find also in the sound a thought,
Hearing it by this distant northern sea.

The sea of faith
Was once, too, at the full, and round earth's shore
Lay like the folds of a bright girdle furl'd.
But now I only hear
Its melancholy, long, withdrawing roar,
Retreating, to the breath
Of the night-wind, down the vast edges drear
And naked shingles of the world.

Ah, love, let us be true
To one another! for the world, which seems
To lie before us like a land of dreams,
So various, so beautiful, so new,
Hath really neither joy, nor love, nor light,
Nor certitude, nor peace, nor help for pain;
And we are here as on a darkling plain
Swept with confused alarms of struggle and flight,
Where ignorant armies clash by night.

Dover Beach, MATTHEW ARNOLD.

When, in disgrace with fortune and men's eyes,
I all alone beweep my outcast state,
And trouble deaf heaven with my bootless cries,
And look upon myself, and curse my fate,
Wishing me like to one more rich in hope,
Featured like him, like him with friends possess'd,
Desiring this man's art and that man's scope,
With what I most enjoy contented least;
Yet in these thoughts myself almost despising,
Haply I think on thee, and then my state,
Like to the lark at break of day arising
From sullen earth, sings hymns at heaven's gate;
For thy sweet love remember'd such wealth brings
That then I scorn to change my state with kings.

Sonnet No. 29, SHAKESPEARE.

Swiftly walk o'er the western wave,
    Spirit of Night!
Out of the misty eastern cave,
Where, all the long and lone daylight,
Thou wovest dreams of joy and fear,
Which make thee terrible and dear,—
    Swift be thy flight!

Wrap thy form in a mantle gray,
    Star-inwrought!
Blind with thine hair the eyes of Day;
Kiss her until she be wearied out,
Then wander o'er city, and sea, and land,
Touching all with thine opiate wand—
    Come, long-sought!

When I arose and saw the dawn,
    I sighed for thee;
When light rode high, and the dew was gone,
And noon lay heavy on flower and tree,

And the weary Day turned to his rest,
Lingering like an unloved guest,
   I sighed for thee.

Thy brother Death came, and cried,
   Wouldst thou me?
Thy sweet child Sleep, the filmy-eyed,
Murmured like a noontide bee,
Shall I nestle near thy side?
Wouldst thou me?—And I replied,
   No, not thee!

Death will come when thou art dead,
   Soon, too soon—
Sleep will come when thou art fled;
Of neither would I ask the boon
I ask of thee, beloved Night—
Swift be thine approaching flight,
   Come soon, soon!

To Night, SHELLEY.

I met a traveller from an antique land
Who said: "Two vast and trunkless legs of stone
Stand in the desert. . . . Near them, on the sand,
Half sunk, a shattered visage lies, whose frown,
And wrinkled lip, and sneer of cold command,
Tell that its sculptor well those passions read
Which yet survive, stamped on these lifeless things,
The hand that mocked them, and the heart that fed:
And on the pedestal these words appear:
'My name is Ozymandias, king of kings:
Look on my works, ye Mighty, and despair!'
Nothing beside remains.   Round the decay
Of that colossal wreck, boundless and bare
The lone and level sands stretch far away."

Ozymandias, SHELLEY.

Though I speak with the tongues of men and of angels, and have not charity, I am become as sounding brass, or a tinkling cymbal.

And though I have the gift of prophecy, and understand all mysteries, and all knowledge; and though I have all faith, so that I could remove mountains, and have not charity, I am nothing.

And though I bestow all my goods to feed the poor, and though I give my body to be burned, and have not charity, it profiteth me nothing.

Charity suffereth long, and is kind; charity envieth not; charity vaunteth not itself, is not puffed up, doth not behave itself unseemly, seeketh not her own, is not easily provoked, thinketh no evil; rejoiceth not in iniquity, but rejoiceth in the truth; beareth all things, believeth all things, hopeth all things, endureth all things.

Charity never faileth: but whether there be prophecies, they shall fail; whether there be tongues, they shall cease; whether there be knowledge, it shall vanish away. For we know in part, and we prophesy in part. But when that which is perfect is come, then that which is in part shall be done away.

When I was a child, I spake as a child, I understood as a child, I thought as a child: but when I became a man, I put away childish things. For now we see through a glass, darkly; but then face to face: now I know in part; but then shall I know even as also I am known.

And now abideth faith, hope, charity, these three; but the greatest of these is charity.

I Corinthians, xiii.

Some people say it is a very easy thing to get up of a cold morning. You have only, they tell you, to take the resolution; and the thing is done. This may be very true; just as a boy at school has only to take a flogging, and the thing is over. But we have not at all made up our minds upon it; and we find it a very pleasant exercise to discuss the matter, candidly, before we get up. This, at least, is not idling, though it may be lying. It affords an excellent answer to those who ask how lying in bed can be indulged in by a reasoning being—a rational creature. How? Why, with the argument calmly at work in one's head, and the clothes over one's shoulder. Oh—it is a fine way of spending a sensible, impartial half-hour. . . .

On my first movement towards the anticipation of getting up I find that such parts of the sheets and bolster as are exposed to the air of the room are stone-cold. On opening my eyes, the first thing that meets them is my own breath rolling forth, as if in the open air, like smoke out of a chimney. Think of this symptom. Then I turn my eyes sideways and see the window all frozen over. Think of that. Then the servant comes in. "It is very cold this morning, is it not?"—"Very cold, sir."—"Very cold indeed, isn't it?"—"Very cold indeed, sir."—"More than usually so, isn't it, even for this weather?" (Here the servant's wit and good nature are put to a considerable test, and the enquirer lies on thorns for the answer.) "Why, sir . . . I think it *is*." (Good creature! There is not a better or more truth-telling servant going.) "I must rise, however—get me some warm water." Here comes a fine interval between the departure of the servant and the arrival of the hot water; during which, of course, it is of "no use?" to get up. The hot water comes. "Is it quite hot?"—"Yes, sir."—"Perhaps too hot for shaving; I must wait a little?"—"No, sir, it will just do." (There is an over-nice propriety sometimes, an officious zeal of virtue, a little troublesome.) "Oh—the shirt—you must air my clean shirt;—linen gets very damp this weather."—"Yes, sir." Here another delicious five minutes. A knock at the door. "Oh, the shirt—very well. My stockings—I think the stockings had better be aired too."—"Very well, sir." Here another interval. At length everything is ready except myself. I now, continues our incumbent (a happy word, by-the-by, for a country vicar)—I now cannot help thinking a good deal—who can?—upon the unnecessary and villainous custom of shaving: it is a thing so unmanly (here I nestle closer)—so effeminate (here I recoil from an unlucky step into the colder part of the bed). . . . think of the razor itself—how totally opposed to every sensation of bed—how cold, how edgy, how hard! how utterly different from anything like the warm and circling amplitude. . . . Add to this, benumbed fingers, which may help you to cut yourself, a quivering body, a frozen towel, and a ewer full of ice. . . .

A money-getter may be drawn out of his bed by three or four pence; but this will not suffice for a student. A proud man may say, "What shall I think of myself, if I don't get up?" but the more humble one will be content to waive this prodigious notion of himself, out of respect to his kindly bed. The mechanical man shall get up without any ado at all; and so shall the barometer. An ingenious lier in bed will find hard matter of discussion even on the score of health and longevity. He will ask us for our proofs and precedents of the ill effects of lying later in cold weather; and sophisticate much on the advantages of an even temperature of body; of the natural propensity (pretty universal) to have one's way; and of the animals that roll themselves up and sleep all the winter. . . .

From *On Getting Up on Cold Mornings*, LEIGH HUNT.

> When in the chronicle of wasted time
> I see descriptions of the fairest wights,
> And beauty making beautiful old rhyme
> In praise of ladies dead and lovely knights,
> Then, in the blazon of sweet beauty's best,
> Of hand, of foot, of lip, of eye, of brow,
> I see their antique pen would have express'd
> Even such a beauty as you master now.

So all their praises are but prophecies
Of this our time, all you prefiguring;
And, for they look'd but with divining eyes,
They had not skill enough your worth to sing:
For we, which now behold these present days,
Have eyes to wonder, but lack tongues to praise.

Sonnet No. 106, SHAKESPEARE.

Othello.

Most potent, grave, and reverend signoirs,
My very noble and approved good masters,
That I have ta'en away this old man's daughter,
It is most true; true, I have married her:
The very head and front of my offending
Hath this extent, no more.   Rude am I in my speech,
And little blest with the soft phrase of peace;
For since these arms of mine had seven years' pith,
Till now some nine moons wasted, they have used
Their dearest action in the tented field;
And little of this great world can I speak,
More than pertains to feats of broil and battle;
And therefore little shall I grace my cause
In speaking for myself.   Yet, by your gracious patience,
I will a round unvarnish'd tale deliver
Of my whole course of love; what drugs, what charms,
What conjuration and what mighty magic—
For such proceeding I am charged withal—
I won his daughter.
Her father loved me, oft invited me,
Still questioned me the story of my life
From year to year, the battles, sieges, fortunes
That I have pass'd.
I ran it through, even from my boyish days
To the very moment that he bade me tell it
Wherein I spake of most disastrous chances,
Of moving accidents by flood and field,
Of hair-breadth 'scapes i' the imminent deadly breach,

Of being taken by the insolent foe,
And sold to slavery, of my redemption thence,
And portance in my travels' history:
Wherein of antres vast and deserts idle,
Rough quarries, rocks, and hills whose heads touch heaven,
It was my hint to speak,—such was the process;
And of the Cannibals that each other eat,
The Anthropophagi, and men whose heads
Do grow beneath their shoulders.   This to hear
Would Desdemona seriously incline:
But still the house-affairs would draw her thence;
Which ever as she could with haste dispatch,
She'd come again, and with a greedy ear
Devour up my discourse: which I observing,
Took once a pliant hour, and found good means
To draw from her a prayer of earnest heart
That I would all my pilgrimage dilate,
Whereof by parcels she had something heard,
But not intentively: I did consent,
And often did beguile her of her tears
When I did speak of some distressful stroke
That my youth suffer'd.   My story being done,
She gave me for my pains a world of sighs:
She swore, in faith, 'twas strange, 'twas passing strange;
'Twas pitiful, 'twas wondrous pitiful:
She wish'd she had not heard it, yet she wish'd
That heaven had made her such a man: she thank'd me,
And bade me, if I had a friend that loved her,
I should teach him how to tell my story,
And that would woo her.   Upon this hint I spake:
She lov'd me for the dangers I had pass'd,
And I lov'd her that she did pity them.
This only is the witchcraft I have used.
Here comes the lady; let her witness it.

From *Othello*, SHAKESPEARE.

There is sweet music here that softer falls
Than petals from blown roses on the grass,
Or night-dews on still waters between walls
Of shadowy granite, in a gleaming pass;
Music that gentlier on the spirit lies,
Than tired eyelids upon tired eyes;
Music that brings sweet sleep down from the blissful skies.
Here are cool mosses deep,
And thro' the moss the ivies creep,
And in the stream the long-leaved flowers weep,
And from the craggy ledge the poppy hangs in sleep.

Why are we weigh'd upon with heaviness,
And utterly consumed with sharp distress,
While all things else have rest from weariness?
All things have rest: why should we toil alone,
We only toil, who are the first of things,
And make perpetual moan,
Still from one sorrow to another thrown;
Nor ever fold our wings,
And cease from wanderings,
Nor steep our brows in slumber's holy balm
Nor harken what the inner spirit sings,
"There is no joy but calm!"—
Why should we only toil, the roof and crown of things?

Lo! in the middle of the wood,
The folded leaf is woo'd from out the bud
With winds upon the branch, and takes no care,
Sun-steep'd at noon, and in the moon
Nightly dew-fed; and turning yellow
Falls, and floats adown the air.
Lo! sweeten'd with the summer light,
The full-juiced apple, waxing over-mellow,
Drops in a silent autumn night.
All its allotted length of days
The flower ripens in its place,
Ripens and fades, and falls, and hath no toil,
Fast-rooted in the fruitful soil.

Hateful is the dark-blue sky,
Vaulted o'er the dark-blue sea.
Death is the end of life; ah, why
Should life all labour be?
Let us alone. Time driveth onward fast,
And in a little while our lips are dumb.
Let us alone. What is it that will last?
All things are taken from us, and become
Portions and parcels of the dreadful past.
Let us alone. What pleasures can we have
To war with evil? Is there any peace
In ever climbing up the climbing wave?
All things have rest, and ripen toward the grave
In silence—ripen, fall, and cease:
Give us long rest or death, dark death, or dreamful ease.

How sweet it were, hearing the downward stream,
With half-shut eyes ever to seem
Falling asleep in a half-dream!
To dream and dream, like yonder amber light,
Which will not leave the myrrh-bush on the height;
To hear each other's whisper'd speech;
Eating the Lotos day by day,
To watch the crisping ripples on the beach,
And tender curving lines of creamy spray;
To lend our hearts and spirits wholly
To the influence of mild-minded melancholy;
To muse and brood and live again in memory,
With those old faces of our infancy
Heap'd over with a mound of grass,
Two handfuls of white dust, shut in an urn of brass!

Dear is the memory of our wedded lives,
And dear the last embraces of our wives
And their warm tears; but all hath suffer'd change;
For surely now our household hearths are cold,
Our sons inherit us, our looks are strange,
And we should come like ghosts to trouble joy.
Or else the island princes over-bold

Have eat our substance, and the minstrel sings
Before them of the ten years' war in Troy,
And our great deeds, as half-forgotten things.
Is there confusion in the little isle?
Let what is broken so remain.
The Gods are hard to reconcile;
'Tis hard to settle order once again.
There *is* confusion worse than death,
Trouble on trouble, pain on pain,
Long labour unto aged breath,
Sore task to hearts worn out by many wars
And eyes grown dim with gazing on the pilot-stars.
But propped on beds of amaranthe and moly,
How sweet—while warm airs lull us, blowing lowly—
With half-dropped eyelid still,
Beneath a heaven dark and holy,
To watch the long bright river drawing slowly
His waters from the purple hill—
To hear the dewy echoes calling
From cave to cave thro' the thick-twined vine—
To watch the emerald-colour'd water falling
Thro' many a woven acanthus-wreath divine!
Only to hear and see the far-off sparkling brine,
Only to hear were sweet, stretch'd out beneath the pine.

The Lotos blooms below the barren peak,
The Lotos blows by every winding creek;
All day the wind breathes low with mellower tone;
Thro' every hollow cave and alley lone
Round and round the spicy downs the yellow Lotos-dust is
    blown.
We have had enough of action, and of motion we,
Roll'd to starboard, roll'd to larboard, when the surge was
    seething free,
Where the wallowing monster spouted his foam-fountains in
    the sea.
Let us swear an oath, and keep it with an equal mind,
In the hollow Lotos-land to live and lie reclined
On the hills, like Gods together, careless of mankind.

For they lie beside their nectar, and the bolts are hurl'd
Far below them in the valleys, and the clouds are lightly
    curl'd
Round their golden houses, girdled with the gleaming world;
Where they smile in secret, looking over wasted lands,
Blight and famine, plague and earthquake, roaring deeps and
    fiery sands,
Clanging fights, and flaming towns, and sinking ships, and
    praying hands.
But they smile, they find a music centred in a doleful song
Steaming up, a lamentation and an ancient tale of wrong,
Like a tale of little meaning tho' the words are strong;
Chanted from an ill-used race of men that cleave the soil,
Sow the seed, and reap the harvest with enduring toil,
Storing yearly little dues of wheat, and wine and oil
Till they perish and they suffer—some 'tis whisper'd—down
    in hell
Suffer endless anguish, others in Elysian valleys dwell,
Resting weary limbs at last on beds of asphodel.
Surely, surely, slumber is more sweet than toil, the shore
Than labour in the deep mid-ocean, wind and wave and oar
O, rest ye, brother mariners, we will not wander more.

Choric Song from the Lotos-eaters, TENNYSON.

BOOKS FOR FURTHER STUDY

COMMUNICATION

"On Human Communication"   Colin Cherry
The M.I.T. Press

PHONETICS

"An Introduction to the Pronunciation of English"
A. C. Gimson   Edward Arnold

PROSODY AND POETICS

"The Anatomy of Poetry"   Marjorie Boulton
Routledge and Kegan Paul

MOVEMENT

"Movement, Voice and Speech"   A. Musgrave
Horner   Methuen

INDEX OF SELECTIONS